A Step-By-Step **Guide** to
Track, and **Expand** Your **Toddler's** **Language**

MY TODDLER'S FIRST W♥RDS

Kimberly O. Scanlon, M.A., CCC-SLP
Author of My Toddler Talks

My Toddler's First Words:
A Step-By-Step Guide to Jump-Start, Track, and Expand Your Toddler's Language

The example situations, questions from parents, and anecdotes that appear throughout this book are inspired by my work as a speech-language pathologist and my life as a parent. Information about individuals has been changed to protect their identity and are, in some instances, composites.

Cover: Rocio Martin Osuna
Layout: Jera Publishing
Illustrations: Rocio Martin Osuna

ISBN: 197837190X
ISBN-13: 9781978371903

Library of Congress Control Number: 2018905026

Printed in the United States of America

Published by:

Ramsey, NJ

A Happy Place for
Speech and **Language**
LEARNING

mytoddlertalks.com

Sign up today to get exclusive access
to informational bonuses, additional
handouts, freebies, and more.

Disclaimer

If you have genuine concerns regarding a child's speech and language skills, please consult a licensed and certified speech-language pathologist for guidance. This workbook is not meant to replace speech therapy. For children in speech therapy, it can be used in conjunction with the recommendations of the treating speech-language pathologist. This book is not intended to, nor could it, take the place of the advice, intervention, or both, from a physician, speech-language pathologist, or early-childhood provider who has evaluated your child in person. It is not speech-language therapy, nor is it a professional assessment of any child's speech and language skills. Kimberly does not guarantee speech/language progress.

Mention of specific companies, organizations, or authorities in this book does not imply endorsement by the author, nor does mention of specific companies, organizations, or authorities imply that they endorse this book or author. Kimberly has made every effort to provide accurate internet addresses and other contact information as of the time of publication. Kimberly does not assume any responsibility for errors or for changes that occur after publication, nor does she have any control over or assume any responsibility for third-party websites or their content.

Contents

Foreword

BECOMING A PARENT is truly life changing — it is beautiful, joyful, and raw. You are given this tiny new life to feed, nurture, guide, support, and teach. You love him or her selflessly and unconditionally. You celebrate your child's milestones and support him or her through the highs, the lows, and everything in between. You wipe tears and noses, bandage skinned knees, and kiss the child's boo-boos. You read the same books over and over again because of the joy it brings your little one. You get to see the world in a whole new way: through the eyes of a child. There is nothing else quite as magical as watching your child grow, learn, and thrive.

I am the lucky mother of four beautiful children. Two of my boys were what we refer to as "late talkers." All areas of their development were on target, or even advanced, with the exception of expressive speech and language. They understood everything that was said to them and could follow complex directions; however, they used very few real words to communicate. As a pediatric speech-language pathologist (yes, even we can have children who struggle with speech!), I was in a unique position: I already had the knowledge and skills to help support and expand my late talkers' language development. However, this is not the case for the hundreds of concerned parents, grandparents, and caregivers who email me each year asking what they can do to help encourage their toddler's speech development.

When you suspect your child may be struggling in some area of development, it can feel like your whole world is collapsing. It can be a very stressful, confusing, and chaotic time. Doctors, specialists, therapists, they all seem to speak in a language that sounds foreign, and it is certainly difficult territory to navigate, especially in the beginning. One can quickly become overwhelmed when trying to find answers. Having a child with chronic illness, I've been there. I've experienced the feelings of confusion, anxiety, fear, frustration, helplessness, and that *need to learn as much as you can* to help your child.

I realized early in my career that I was not going to be making as much of an impact on the children I was working with as their own parents could—if they just had the skills. I spent about sixty minutes a week with each child, whereas their parents were with them the remaining 167 hours or so. This became even more abundantly clear to me when I had my own late talkers. I was able to support them 24-7 because I had the knowledge and skills to do so. Knowledge is power. I knew I could help parents help their children if I could just teach them how. This inspired me to start my blog several years ago in an effort to share my expertise and provide education, inspiration, and empowerment to parents of young children with speech and language delays.

This passion for empowering parents with knowledge is what brought Kim and me together several years ago. We were both writing to the same audience on our blogs, and she was working on her first book, *My Toddler Talks*. We quickly bonded over our belief that equipping parents and caregivers with as much information as possible is one of our primary goals as pediatric speech-language pathologists working with families of young children. We both felt compelled to write and share our expertise with others in hopes to make a broader impact on the lives of young children and their families.

As a parent, I also understand it's difficult to find the time to read books and search the internet for accurate and helpful information. This is one of the beauties of *My Toddler's First Words*. Kim provides parents with clear and concise information based on her decade of experience coaching paired with the most current research in the field of speech-language pathology. No need to spend hours on the internet trying to deduce fact from fiction and sort through all the fluff and noise. *My Toddler's First Words* provides parents and caregivers with accurate guidelines on typical speech and language development and thoroughly explains how to implement strategies that support naturalistic development of speech and language skills. All of this information is provided in a unique, interactive workbook format to help you formulate goals, plan strategies, and evaluate your child's progress. Professionals will also find this an excellent resource to use with the families they work with.

My Toddler's First Words is for the parent or caregiver who is concerned about his or her child's speech and language development and wants to take a hands-on approach to supporting his or her child. As Kim explains in her introduction, this book is not a replacement for early-intervention services or speech therapy. Clearly, if you are concerned about your child's development, you should not hesitate to contact a professional directly. Knowledge truly is power. The more you know, the more you can support your child. *My Toddler's First Words* will give you the knowledge and power to help your child thrive.

Katie Yeh, MA, CCC-SLP
Founder & Author of *Playing with Words 365*
San Francisco, California

Introduction

I REMEMBER THE FIRST time it happened. A mom showed me her list—the list of all the words or word attempts her daughter had ever said. This parent had diligently recorded anything and everything her daughter had uttered. It was a relatively short list and consisted of sounds and words like *ma*, *da*, *ba*, *baba* for *bottle*, and *shhhh*.

In the subsequent years of working as a pediatric speech-language pathologist, I have continued to encounter many parents who write lists, keep journals, or make mental notes examining and monitoring their children's language development. Some parents have shown me typed, color-coded, dated lists, other parents have shown me lists on random scraps of paper, and several have intentionally observed and remembered new words spoken by their children. Regardless of how organized or spontaneous the collection method, all these parents and caregivers had this in common: a dedication and thirst for knowledge motivated by a concern their child's language *might* be delayed compared to his or her peers. These parents yearned to teach their children first words and wanted their vocabularies to grow and flourish. With their children's attainment of first words, these parents realized they could unlock their children's minds, reduce frustration, and further drive language development.

Parents are essential in developing their children's language skills because they can consistently provide a rich language environment and early language stimulation. The numbers and types of words spoken to children during their first few years of life, a critical period of growth, are vital to their future success. In the 1980s, social scientists Dr. Betty Hart and Dr. Todd Risley published groundbreaking research revealing that early language stimulation and access to a language-rich environment led to later educational achievement. They discovered that how parents talk to their children greatly improves the children's outcomes. With the proper support and resources, parents and caregivers can enhance their children's language-learning development (Woods, Wilcox, Friedman & Murch, 2011).

Knowing parents are vital to their children's success, while experiencing firsthand that motivated parents are thirsty for ways to grow their children's language, I wrote my first book, *My Toddler Talks: Strategies and Activities to Promote Your Child's Language Development*. The book has taught thousands of readers how to use recognized techniques and play routines to facilitate early language development. This next book, *My Toddler's First Words: A Step-By-Step Guide to Jump-Start, Track, and Expand Your Toddler's Language*, can be used alone or in conjunction with *My Toddler Talks*.

This book was written to help parents, like you, learn fundamental concepts to jump-start the tracking and growth of their toddler's first words. Coincidentally, while *My Toddler's First Words* was written primarily for parents, fellow speech-language pathologists and other professionals who are coaching and training parents in clinics or through state-run early-intervention programs have also found it to be extremely useful. Professionals who read earlier versions of *My Toddler's First Words* greatly appreciated the cited research to support their own efforts and recommendations. Many also said that the journaling portion was a powerful way to encourage parents to be more mindful of how they implement the strategies. Additionally, they liked that this book made their sessions a bit easier because parents could jot down questions or discuss points they may have otherwise forgotten to ask or mention at their child's last session.

The coaching and advice I offer in this book grew out of my clinical experiences over the past ten years in combination with evidence-based peer-reviewed research. Please know this book is not a replacement for speech therapy or early-intervention services. It is an outlet, a tool, and a reference to empower and educate you. Despite my best efforts, I will probably not be able to address in this book every concern or question you have. However, one of my major goals is to help you feel good about yourself and your child. This is because *My Toddler's First Words* should give you some competence and confidence in facilitating spoken first words from your toddler.[1]

This interactive book has four parts. The first part, Toddler Language Development Basics, provides information on emerging language development. If you have ever wondered why a toddler is more likely to say "mama" or "doggy" or "uh-oh" instead of mother or ostrich or Jiminy Cricket, then this chapter's for you. Knowing how and why toddlers learn to say first words will empower you to select appropriate ones to target and set realistic expectations. In part two, Analyze Your Toddler's Language, you informally study your toddler's language. Using the worksheets in this part, I'll carefully direct you to reflect and consider your toddler's language, needs, and wants within the context of your family dynamic. Completing these worksheets may take some time, but going through the process will help you to best

---

1 If you are significantly struggling to communicate with your toddler, I highly recommend working with a speech-language pathologist who can model the techniques and provide further expertise. You may want to use this workbook in unison with working with a certified and licensed pediatric speech-language pathologist who specializes in assessing and treating toddlers. These pediatric speech-language pathologists are in a unique position to help because they have years of graduate education and have obtained many clinical hours. They can provide an objective and educated perspective and share additional professional expertise. In some cases, augmentative and alternative communication strategies (AAC) and devices may be recommended. AAC techniques are beyond the scope of this workbook.

understand and serve your toddler and family. The third part of this book, Get Your Toddler Talking, teaches you how to facilitate language development. Not only do I share eight evidence-based techniques, but I also provide tips on how to create a language-rich environment and troubleshooting suggestions for those times when your toddler does not want to say the chosen target word. Though I strived to make the information straightforward and rich with examples to ease learning, you may have to reread certain sections, particularly the techniques portion. I encourage you to do this because rereading is an effective way to better understand new information. The last part of this guide, Make It Happen, includes an interactive 30-Day Workbook. This workbook was created to inspire you to establish a regular practice to reflect on your efforts in stimulating your toddler's language. I purposefully designed this 30-Day Workbook with busy parents and professionals in mind. The daily questions are consistent to keep you focused on the goals at hand. Only a few lines are provided for your response, as I wanted to make this journal section a no-fuss record keeper.

The term *toddler* is derived from the word *toddle*, meaning to move with short, unsteady steps (Merriam-Webster, 2018). Toddlers are young children whose ages span between twelve and thirty-six months old. Throughout this book, I interchange the terms *toddler* and *child*. I have done this as a way to sensitively include older-aged children. I also interchange the terms *parent* and *caregiver*, as many readers may be other dedicated family members, nannies, babysitters, or additional members of the child's social network. Also, masculine and feminine pronouns have been alternated to be inclusive.

I'm happy you have found this book. I hope *My Toddler's First Words: A Step-By-Step Guide to Jump-Start, Track, and Expand Your Toddler's Language* gives you a sense of pride in knowing you are actively helping your child reach for the stars.

Enjoy this language-learning journey.

Kimberly Scanlon, MA, CCC-SLP

How to Use This Step-By-Step Guide

BEFORE YOU BEGIN, remember your toddler is unique, and your family dynamic is special. What works for one toddler or family may not work for another. This book provides guidance and gives flexibility in designing an individualized approach for your special toddler. Use these worksheets, suggestions, and techniques to best meet the needs of your toddler and family.[2]

As mentioned in the introduction, *My Toddler's First Words* is divided into four parts. All four parts are equally important and to walk away most informed, you should read the entire book, complete the worksheets, and finish the 30-Day Workbook. However, I realize that people are busy, especially parents. Therefore, I'm sharing a comprehensive, ideal approach; alter it to best fit your life. Some practical and motivational tips to get the most from this book are also included. If you are extremely pressed for time and are willing to forgo the full experience, jump in headfirst and go straight to the techniques section.

➡ Toddler Language Development Basics. Begin by reading part one. Take your time and reread sections as necessary. If this is your first time reading about toddler language, some of the information may seem dense. You are not reading this content to become an expert in the field. You are reading this information to better understand your toddler and to jump-start her first words. Thus, read to obtain a general grasp of why and how toddlers use first words to communicate. Once you think you have a pretty good understanding of the content here, move onto the second part.

---

2   Each worksheet is reproducible for personal use and is also available as a digital download for readers who have purchased this book by visiting www.mytoddlertalks.com and clicking on Members Only Resources.

➤ Analyze Your Toddler's Language. To the best of your ability, complete the worksheets in part two. The answers to questions like "What is my toddler saying?" or "What is my toddler trying to tell me?" are not always straightforward. When a toddler is not yet talking, often you have to assume his intentions. Once your toddler learns words to better convey his intentions, there is less guessing. Follow the specific instructions in this part to guide you.

➤ Get Your Toddler Talking. For part three, read through the different strategies and digest them. Some parents like to read one technique at a time, while others like to read a few or all of them in one sitting. Do what best suits your learning style. Envision using the techniques with your toddler.

➤ Make It Happen. After you have finished reading parts one to three, begin the 30-Day Workbook. This is where everything comes together. This workbook will help you to implement and record how you used the techniques over a thirty-day period. Questions to generate reflections and thoughts are included, as are inspirational quotes, additional tips, and insightful research findings. The instructions on how to use the 30-Day Workbook are on pages 76.

Tips for Getting the Most from This Book

➤ Actively read *My Toddler's First Words*. Break out your pens and highlighters and dive into this book. Write in the book, dog-ear the pages, underline, highlight, circle, and summarize important points. Make reading an active experience so you can retain what you have read.

➤ Keep your copy nearby. Keep it in your purse, suitcase, glove compartment, or on your nightstand or kitchen table or even in the bathroom. If *My Toddler's First Words* is within reach, you're more likely to read it when you have a few minutes.

➤ Have your spouse, a significant other, or another person who is involved in your toddler's care read this book too. Reading with a confidant, who knows your little one, will allow you to discuss the content and collaborate. Depending on the composition of your village, these confidants may also include a grandparent or nanny. Have this same person help you to complete the worksheets. Two heads are better than one.

➽ The list of Common First Words as well as the worksheets in part two are download-able from my free resource library that can be found at mytoddlertalks.com. Download and print these sheets and display them so you can easily and quickly record and track your toddler's language. Most readers like posting the sheets on their fridge or keeping them in their purses, pockets or wallets so they can write something down on the spur of the moment.

PART ONE

Toddler Language Development Basics

Important Questions to Ask

AS WE BEGIN your toddler's language-learning journey, here are some questions to consider:

1 How does your toddler respond to and interact with you?

2 How does your toddler communicate?

3 What is a word?

4 How many words does your toddler say?

5 What types of words does your toddler say?

6 How does your toddler use words to communicate?

7 How fast is your toddler adding words to his or her repertoire?

If you are struggling to answer these questions, keep reading. This book will help you answer them and many more.

1. How does your toddler respond to and interact with you?

Being a mother and working with children on a regular basis, I am skilled at observing how toddlers, such curious beings, seek their parents' attention and yearn to share an experience with them. The image below shows a toddler trying to gain her mother's attention. This toddler desperately wants her mother to see the butterfly fluttering next to them. She is thinking, "Mommy, you need to see this cool thing!" Notice how the toddler is pointing to the butterfly while trying to get her mother's attention.

How your toddler responds to what you say and do is equally important. In this image, a garbage truck is coming down the street and a father, knowing his son *loves* garbage trucks, enthusiastically shouts, "Alex, look! A garbage truck!" Alex responds to his father's exclamation, and immediately stops playing in the dirt to longingly gaze at this amazing vehicle that makes loud noises and eats trash.

The children in these two examples are demonstrating what is called joint or shared attention. This is when two individuals intentionally pay attention to an object or event and they each check to see that the other is paying attention. They are sharing an experience together. Shared attention is a major developmental milestone and is considered a pre-requisite to the onset of language. Typically, it emerges by twelve months of age. Sharing an experience is vital to building bonds and learning language. It is very difficult to understand, communicate, and interact with others if you

cannot share an experience with them. Attending to someone or something in a coordinated fashion provides opportunities to learn language, discern what others are feeling, and assess the world around you. Children who readily respond to their parents' questions and regularly check back in with mommy or daddy to see if they delighted in his or her wonder and interests will have an easier time acquiring language than those who seem to lack these abilities.

As young toddlers, both of my children eagerly pointed to whatever they thought was remarkable or amazing, such as a bird, leaf, or dog. Not only that, but also they always looked at me to make sure I was seeing the thing striking their fancy. They may not have been saying any of these words yet, but they wanted to share the experience with me.

Does your toddler pay attention to you and what is happening in her environment? Does she respond to her name when you call to her? Can she follow your gaze and look where you are looking? When she is excited about something, does she want to share the experience with you? When she is crying or upset, does she somehow tell you what is wrong? If you are answering no to many of these questions, I strongly suggest improving these foundational skills before targeting verbal word production. Please see "Receptive Language Development Tips," table 2, on page 22 for additional information. The following three techniques—identify and appreciate the child's lead, be responsive, and imitate, imitate, imitate—in part three of this book are helpful in developing these skills too.

2. How does your toddler communicate?

One night at around 6:00 p.m., when my son was about fourteen months old, he intentionally told me, using an elaborate sequence of nonverbal actions, that he wanted to sleep. First, he looked at me, ensuring he had my attention. Then he laid down on the living room carpet and pretended to sleep. I saw this and said, "Oh, you want to go to sleep?" To which, he smiled. Next, he walked over to the couch where his sleep sack was located, picked it up, and gave it to me. Then immediately, he extended his hands up, gesturing that he wanted to be picked up. Once I scooped him up, he rested his head on my shoulder. Even though he did not say any words, he communicated that he was tired and ready for bed.

When your toddler is hungry, what does he do? Does he take you by the hand, leading you to the refrigerator in the kitchen? Does he point to what he wants to eat? Does he look at you to make sure you understand him? Does he use any gestures, facial expressions, or body movements to convey what he wants? Does he make any sounds? Does he use any sign language? Does he try to say a word? Or does your toddler cry and scream when he is hungry because he doesn't know how to intentionally communicate? Knowing how your toddler communicates will help you to better understand his world and set realistic expectations for progress. If your little one resorts to pulling you to what he wants or cries and screams out of frustration, see pages 25, "Question from a Parent" for additional information.

3. What is a word?

Let's begin by defining a word.

Dr. Erika Hoff, professor and director of the Language Development Lab at Florida Atlantic University, defines a word as "a sound sequence that symbolizes meaning and can stand alone" (Hoff, 2005, p. 422). The meaning of this sound sequence must also be consistent. For instance, a toddler will say, "Ball," or an approximation of the word (e.g., "baw") every time she sees her favorite red, bouncy ball.

A dog barking, a baby crying, and a cat meowing may convey meaning, but these sounds are not symbols, and therefore, they are not words. To use words, toddlers must realize words are symbols to represent concepts. Thus, a random sound not used consistently to refer to one person, place, or thing is not considered a word. But if your child says, "Moo," every time he sees a cow, then that sound can be considered a first word. Or if your child says, "Dodo," every time he sees the family dog, then *dodo* can be considered a first word.

Additionally, and very importantly, a child who is just beginning to talk makes mistakes! These mistakes are paramount to the language-learning process. He may begin by randomly assigning sounds to certain items. These sounds may not be articulated correctly, fully understood, or intelligible to you. Your child may even overuse or overextend a word like *dog* by calling all four-legged animals "dog." With time, practice, and loving encouragement, he will begin to consistently assign certain sounds and words to the proper items.

> ### Question from a Parent
>
> "What exactly is a word? Do sounds count? My kids say sounds that have meanings to them. Do they count as words?"
>
> —Joe, father of thirty-four-month-old twins

4. How many words does your toddler say?

The answer is pretty straightforward. It consists of the number of words your toddler can independently and spontaneously say without any help or support.

How easily can your child use words during spur-of-the-moment conversations and interactions? For instance, Willie says, "Milk," every time he wants milk and doesn't need to be prompted to say it. He also says, "Wawa," when he wants water instead of milk.

The quantity of words in your child's vocabulary is important for a few reasons.

Delayed or missed communication milestones may indicate potential difficulty in your child's development. Children who are later diagnosed with specific language impairment, autism, and other

> The quantity of words in your child's vocabulary is only one piece of the puzzle.

learning disorders are often slow to say first words and combine words together. This is not meant to alarm you, as each child is unique and develops at his own pace. Awareness and recognition of delays should propel you to take action, as early intervention can change the course of a child's development and increase the chances of improvement.

A larger vocabulary size also correlates to the ability to say more speech sounds and produce words with complex sound combinations. First words usually contain a limited number of speech sounds and have simple syllable structures. For instance, "mama", "dada," and "wawa" each contain one repeated syllable. As a child's vocabulary grows, he eventually says words with nonreduplicated syllables. *Mama* turns into *mommy*, *dada* evolves into *daddy*, and *wawa* progresses to *water*.

A limited vocabulary may impede communication, too. Have you ever had a moment when you struggled to find the right word to say or couldn't retrieve a word? It was probably frustrating. It may have even interfered with your conversation. Imagine being a toddler who is just learning to speak. You have a small vocabulary and often use one word to represent more than one thing. You call all men "dada," sometimes even your mommy. You say, "Apple," when you really want an orange. You scream at the top of your lungs when mommy gives you your toy truck, because even though you said "twuck," you really wanted your school bus. These inaccurate uses of words are known as over-extensions, and they are common in early vocabulary development. Over-extensions decrease as toddlers learn new words. With experience and exposure, a toddler will typically learn the names of his favorite items and people. Consequently, communication becomes more effective. The toddler, who wanted the school bus, now confidently says, "Bus," instead of "twuck," and successfully gets what he wants. Effective communication results in less interpreting and less guessing and more understanding. There may be times when you still have to decipher your toddler's actions and read the situation and guess what she is telling you. This is expected. Communication breakdowns even happen with well-spoken adults.

Lastly, a larger expressive vocabulary makes navigating the world much easier. Once you can understand and use a word, the brain is free to spend its resources learning more words or focusing on higher-level language tasks such as processing and creating word combinations.

5. What types of words does your toddler say?

Variety is the spice of life. This applies to language, too.

We want our toddlers to use an arsenal of different *types* of words. Some of these include the following:

- Action words or verbs (e.g., *eat, sleep, done*)

- Describing words or adjectives (e.g., *big, hot, yucky*)

- Early location words or prepositions (e.g., *in, up, there*)

- Names of persons, places, or things or nouns (e.g., *nose, choo-choo, dada or daddy*).

- Social words (e.g., *hi, bye, uh-oh, what's that?*)

Targeting various types of words will allow your toddler to explore the relationship between words, paving the way to future word combinations and sentences. Action words or verbs are particularly important because every sentence requires a verb. Children begin to say early sentences when they start to say verbs. Research findings suggest that a greater diversity of verbs improves later grammatical development as well as the ability to formulate a variety of sentences (Hadley, Rispoli & Ning, 2016). Karen Jacobsen, speech language pathologist and clinical instructor at the Department of Speech and Hearing Sciences at the University of Washington, advocates for targeting verbs early on because verbs help the toddler to better control or regulate her environment (Lederer, 2018). Rather than crying because your toddler is hungry, she can say, "eat" to request that she wants to eat. Or, if she is thirsty she can say, "drink" to request that she wants to drink.

Adjectives are also useful in communication exchanges because they help to differentiate one item, or group of items, from another (e.g., "That is a *dirty* sock. This is a *clean* sock. Let's put on the *dirty* sock in the laundry basket").

> Expressive vocabulary refers to the words a person can express or communicate through talking, writing, signing, or other augmentative and alternative means.

6. How does your toddler use words to communicate?

Language gives us the unlimited ability to communicate our thoughts, feelings, and needs. It also allows us to tell others about what we see and experience. Not too long ago, a twenty-nine-month-old toddler and her mother came to me for speech therapy. Let's call this girl Samantha. According to her mother, Samantha said many words and talked all the time. Her mother wasn't concerned about the number of words in Samantha's vocabulary. She even thought Samantha wouldn't qualify for services because she said so many words. However, despite Samantha's ability to reel off a long list of words, her mother worried because it didn't seem like Samantha was using her words to properly express herself. It was nearly impossible to have a real conversation with Samantha. She rarely answered questions and never used the words to tell her parents what she wanted. As a result, Samantha had many tantrums and her parents were very frustrated.

We want our children to be social communicators who can tell us their needs and wants, ask questions, and convey their thoughts in an easy-to-understand manner. Table 1 lists some various types of communicative functions. These are the different reasons or purposes for why we communicate with one another. The toddler who can name every car brand, train, or extinct dinosaur may have a lot of nouns in his expressive vocabulary, but how is he using these words? Is he rattling them off in a parrot-fashion, like Samantha, or is he using them to make a request or to share a comment?

A child excitedly shouting and pointing to "T-Rex!" while looking at his mom is conveying to his mom that she *has to* look at this dinosaur. He is demanding attention and shared enjoyment.

A child who says "T-Rex?" with rising intonation, sounding like he is asking a question, while placing the toy dinosaur into your shopping cart is requesting that you buy T-Rex.

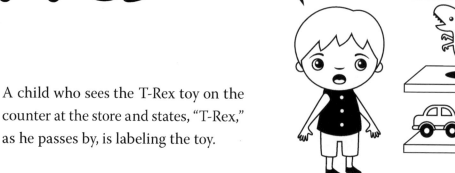

A child who sees the T-Rex toy on the counter at the store and states, "T-Rex," as he passes by, is labeling the toy.

TABLE 1: **Types of Communication Functions**

PURPOSE OF COMMUNICATION	EXAMPLES
Request	"I want..."
Reject or protest	"No!"
Label	"That's a _____."
Comment	"Hot. That's hot."
Ask questions	"What is that?"
Socially interact	"Hi!" "Bye!"

Some parents initially find it difficult to discern between labeling and commenting. When a child uses a word as a label, it means the child is simply naming something or someone. Commenting is more social in nature because it involves expressing an opinion or sharing a reaction. Ask, "What is my child trying to tell me? Is there a purpose to her words?" If she is primarily labeling objects and not using words to intentionally communicate various functions, then it wise to target words to meet these lacking communicative needs.

If your child is getting easily frustrated because she cannot open a box, you may want to target words like "open" or "help". If your child attempts to dangerously climb the counters in search of food, perhaps you need to teach him or her "eat". If your child starts crying when she can't convey the need or burning desire to have one more block, one more cookie, or one more turn at play, perhaps you need her to learn the word "more". Using words to request something or someone, and likewise to reject something or someone, are usually the first types of communication functions speech-language pathologists target when increasing a toddler's first-word repertoire. I further explain this in the section "Selecting Appropriate First Words to Target" (on page 20).

7. How fast is your toddler adding words to his or her repertoire?

Typically, toddlers add new words to their vocabularies on a regular basis. How else would they go from having between two to six words at one year old to one thousand words by three years old?

By tracking your toddler's words, you are more inclined to notice the pace of his vocabulary growth. If you notice his vocabulary is not progressing as it should, this may persuade you to contact a professional, like a speech-language pathologist, to assist you. It is worth repeating that it is particularly important to monitor the growth of action words or verbs. Studies suggest that children who have late acquisition of verbs and a slower rate of acceleration in acquiring verbs, from twenty-one to thirty months old, are at increased risk for language impairment. A slower growth pattern is "atypical" for this developmental period (Hadley et al., 2016).

Question from a Parent

My eighteen-month-old only says, "Mama," and, "Dada," and she uses these words whenever she wants anything. We would really like her to start using words to tell us what she wants. I'm encouraging her to use the sign for more. However, her new speech therapist told me to stop trying to have Susie to say the word more. I don't understand why? Her speech therapist couldn't really explain it.

—Father of Susie, an eighteen-month-old

TEACHING TODDLERS TO request by using the sign for *more* (e.g., tapping fingertips together), or saying the word or an approximation of the word, is hotly debated in the speech-therapy circle.

There are some speech-language pathologists who support teaching the word *more* for a couple of reasons. They believe it is a powerful word that can be used in many contexts. Also, it is relatively easy word to say because it is a monosyllable word beginning with an early developing sound ("m"). Additionally, *more* is a word that emerges early in a typical toddler's expressive vocabulary (see the List of Common First Words).

Speech therapists who prefer not to teach the word may refrain because they have witnessed children overusing *more,* so much that it results in lost opportunities to learn new words and apply specific ones. These therapists think that *more* then becomes an empty and ambiguous word.

Regardless of how passionate a speech therapist may feel on this matter, there is one very important thing to know about the word *more*—it is a word that marks recurrence. This means that something or some action is wanted again. Therefore, *more* is *not* an initial request and should not be used *before* the child has actually had what he desired. For example, if a child wants a cookie, he should say *cookie,* not *more* for the initial request. He should only say "more" or "more cookie" once he has already had a cookie. Thus, when introducing or eliciting the word *more,* one must remember that *more* should only be used after he has received a desired object or action. Also, while *more* does emerge relatively early, by approximately 20 months of age for most toddlers, it is not one of the first five to ten words that toddlers typically say. Other words like mommy, daddy, shoe, hi, up, and dog, are usually spoken before the word *more* (Lederer, 2018a).

Since I offer highly individualized speech therapy and use many naturalistic language-modeling and elicitation techniques, there are times when I introduce the word *more* earlier than other times. It depends on the child and the context. If I was playing with a child and he wanted more of something, I would say and encourage the word *more*, as it is the most natural and expected word based on the situation and need. I do not teach words or signs in isolation or in a drill-like format. I also do not teach *more* to be used as a general request. For instance, a child is hungry and says, "More," because he remembers that the last time he said *more*, mommy gave him apple slices. In this case, the child is possibly overextending the word to mean he wants something to eat. For this child, I would encourage him to learn high-frequency words related to eating, drinking, and favorite food items. However, this child's overextension of *more* gives us insight into how he is thinking. These happy accidents allow us to better understand how a child thinks and processes language.

Selecting Appropriate First Words to Target

WE WANT TO target first words that will give your toddler the most reward for her effort—words that are fun, functional, and meaningful.

Functional communication occurs when a child uses words to express a basic need, want, or thought. If your child is not functionally communicating and there is frustration, it is best to use a systematic method of teaching first words (Sigafoos et al., 2004).

A systematic approach to selecting first words entails targeting ones that will be

1   understood and recognized by the toddler,

2   used to make requests,

3   used to reject or protest something or someone,

4   heard or can be attempted frequently throughout the day, and

5   motivating and interesting to the toddler and special to the family.

Suggestions for Selecting First Words to Target

1. Words that can be understood and recognized by the toddler

Typically, before children begin to say or use a word, they usually understand what the word means. Receptive language is the ability to understand words. Expressive language is the ability to use words to express needs, wants, and ideas. Choose words that your toddler is more likely to understand based on his or her abilities and age. For instance, most toddlers have an easier time understanding basic and general words like, "good" or "yummy" versus more specific words like "favorite"or "delicious".

If you have concerns about your child's receptive-language ability or notice he has difficulty pointing to pictures in a book, understanding simple questions, or following simple directions (e.g., "Haley, point to the dog," or "Sloane, where is your book?" or "Sam, give me a hug."), it may mean that your child needs more support to understand. Young children will be exposed to many new words they do not understand at first. Your toddler's understanding will increase with repeated exposure to the word and with your guidance and support. The main point is to choose words that make sense to your toddler and to provide additional support when needed. There are several ways to enhance your child's ability to learn and understand new words. Please see table 2 on page 22 for some ideas. Creating a language-rich environment also drives both receptive- and expressive-language development. Please see "How to Create a Language-Rich Environment" (on page 67) for suggestions.

Food for Thought

The more severe the delay or disability (e.g., children diagnosed with autism or cerebral palsy), the longer it usually takes to attain the functional communication skills of requesting and rejecting. Often, the less severe the delay, the easier it is to functionally communicate. If your child has made good gains in verbally requesting and rejecting, then move on to increasing his or her expressive vocabulary. However, regardless of the child's severity level or disability, we should always strive to create a language-rich environment. This is because children with more severe delays sometimes are spoken to less, further reducing their ability to learn new words. Every child deserves access to a language-rich environment. For more tips on how to create this, please see "How to Create a Language-Rich Environment" on page 67.

TABLE 2: Receptive Language Development Tips

1. **Get your child's attention.** Minimize background noise and distractions. Obtain your child's eye contact and encourage face-to-face communication before giving a direction, asking a question, or requiring participation in an activity. If your child struggles to make eye contact, make looking at you simply irresistible. Show him or her something interesting and say, "Look!" Do this by keeping close proximity to your child; bend down, stand close or sit near, and position the interesting object close to your face. Do this in a loving and gentle manner.

2. **Incorporate multiple ways to facilitate understanding.** Use gestures, pictures, facial expressions, and body language to further express meaning or to demonstrate a concept, idea, or direction.

3. **Speak using grammatically correct sentences.** Talk to your child throughout the day and during your daily routines. Use simple but grammatically correct and complete sentences. Instead of saying, "Dog big!" Say, an entire sentence, "That dog is big!" Hearing the grammatical elements of a sentence accelerates children's understanding and makes it easier for them to learn the rules of grammar.

4. **Say, emphasize, and repeat new vocabulary words.** Explain and describe what you and your child are doing, seeing, feeling, touching, and smelling. Purposefully make connections between what your toddler is currently seeing or experiencing to other meaningful and relevant situations or past events. Repeat new vocabulary words so your child can hear the words and be exposed to them numerous times.

   → Verb learning tip: Say the verb immediately before performing the action or before the toddler performs the action. (e.g., "Roll. I'll roll the ball," or, "Push. You're pushing the cart.")

   → Adjective learning tip: Use objects with contrasting features to make the differences more noticeable. For instance, show your child a small ball and say, "This is a small ball," and then show your child a big ball and say, "This is a big ball."

5. **Play.** Regularly play with your child and infuse your play routines with language. How your child plays is indicative of how he or she thinks. Interactive play routines that are child led and adult facilitated provide a practical way to model and use words in a playful manner.

2. Words that are used to make requests

Requesting is the ability to appropriately ask for something or for someone to do something—it is one of the earliest communication functions to emerge in toddlers and thus is developmentally appropriate (Carpenter, Mastergeorge & Coggins, 1983). Requesting assistance with something a child cannot do should be targeted first, as should words that help the child request his or her favorite activities, actions, toys, food, people, and so on. Requesting something or someone that is desirable is highly motivating for a child. If saying a word leads to obtaining something she wants, the child is more likely to say the word (A University Center for Excellence in Developmental Disabilities Education, Research, and Service, n.d.).

3. Words that are used to reject or protest something or someone

When children do not have words to escape, avoid, or reject undesired objects, activities, food, certain people, or social interactions, they can act out in frustration by hitting, biting, pinching, or shoving or pushing aside undesired items and people (Sigafoos et al., 2004). First words should be ones that replace a bad behavior (e.g., hitting or biting), reduce frustration (e.g., crying or whining), or replace a socially stigmatizing behavior (e.g., shoving, pushing, or throwing an item the child does not want). Targeting words like *no, stop,* and *all done* are helpful in reducing frustration and replacing undesirable behaviors. The youngest sibling who has to constantly deal with having his toys taken away by an older sister, may need to be taught the empowering word, "Stop" so he doesn't immediately resort to biting, hitting, or pushing his big sister. Teaching a toddler to say "all done", or even to sign this word, will allow him to tell you that he is finished eating and does not want any more peas. The image below shows an example of a child who has learned to sign all done when he has finished an activity.

Targeting words used to reject can be concurrent with targeting words used to request. For instance, if mealtimes are particularly stressful, you can encourage your child to say no to the pasta but request cheese by saying, "Cheese." Always think: Replace the unacceptable with something acceptable. We want our children to use language to reject what they do not want and request what they do want. When this happens, make sure to positively reinforce your child with praise and the preferred item, activity, or person when appropriate.

4. Words that are heard or can be attempted frequently throughout the day

There are many words that naturally repeat throughout our day. Think how often you say hi, bye, in, on, up, out, get, go, or no in a regular day. Many times. Repeating words during a daily routine or strategically repeating certain words during a play routine, (e.g., "baby" or "sleep" while playing with dolls) will drive language learning in toddlers. Repetition gives developing brains frequent exposure and access to multiple opportunities to practice listening to and saying the target word. Good, focused practice leads to acquisition and mastery. Toddlers' language improves when they have a chance to repeatedly practice. Inconsistent or occasional practice will not result in optimal progress (Woods et al., 2011). Furthermore, recent studies show that repeating a new word in successive sentences helps toddlers learn new words faster (Schwab & Lew-Williams, 2016). So do not be afraid to repeat yourself (e.g., "See the *worm*? There's the *worm*. It's a slimy *worm*.").

5. Words that are motivating and interesting to the toddler and special to the family

Toddlers like talking about what interests them. As mentioned before, words that enable children to request favorite activities, actions, toys, food, people, and so on should be targeted first, as should words that help them request assistance with something they cannot do; these specific words are motivating. For instance, if your toddler loves to play peekaboo or a game of chase, then name this highly desirable play routine and encourage your toddler to request it by name. Completing the worksheet "Words That Are Important to My Toddler and Special to Our Family" (on page 42) will help you decide what words to target.

Question from a Parent

Our toddler has gotten into this habit of pulling us to or handing us the things she wants without actually saying or making any sounds when she wants it. If we don't give her what she wants, she starts screaming and crying. I don't want to reward the screaming behavior. I want to encourage her to speak. I'm a little stuck.

—Mother of Mary, a twenty-two-month-old

BEFORE CHILDREN START saying their first words, they typically begin to communicate by using certain gestures, sounds, or body movements. For instance, they may pull you to something, show you a toy, or raise their hands to be picked up. These are known as prelinguistic or presymbolic gestures. In typical development, prelinguistic gestures progress to symbolic gestures and then to verbal language. Symbolic gestures consist primarily of hand movements that carry meaning and are understood by a particular culture. Consequently, they can be used to replace words. Symbolic gestures may represent actions or objects, express comments, convey requests, or facilitate social interactions. Some examples include a thumbs-up, the "shhh" gesture, a pointing finger, an "I dunno" shrug, and a high five.

Toddlers who cannot yet speak may continue to pull you to what they want or hand items to you for some of the following reasons:

1. This basic, nonsymbolic mode of communication has been effective in the past.

Children may use more basic modes of communication because they have had success with them in the past. For instance, your toddler pulls you to the refrigerator and you assume she wants to eat or drink, so you give her a favorite snack. She hands you a windup toy and you assume she wants you to wind it up. Notice how I'm using the word *assume*. When children cannot yet use symbolic gestures, signs, or words to effectively communicate, the communication partner (you) must often assume what they need or want. If your child's needs and wants are easily being met and anticipated by you, there is less incentive for him to use language.

2. They do not yet understand that certain gestures, signs, and words are symbols and have meaning.

If children are not yet communicating or are struggling to, it is not because they are stubborn; they need some support. Gain their attention and assign meaning to their action, gesture, or sound, however random it may seem to you. If children have not been introduced to new gestures, signs, sounds, or words, they will not know what else to do. We must provide them with new ways to communicate via gestures, signs, sounds, and words to replace the pulling, grabbing, crying, and handing over of items.

In Mary's case, next time she pulls you to the fridge, bend down, look at her, and with obvious intention and purpose, point to the fridge and say, "Eat? You want to eat?" Then open the fridge door. Do this each time Mary brings you to the fridge. Take her hand and encourage her to point to the fridge too. Open the fridge as soon as she tries to point to it. Pointing paves the way for future language development. If you are consistent, she will begin to understand that what she does and says has meaning and causes others to react. If your child does not pay attention to your efforts or is not making eye contact and not responding to your interactive exchanges, a referral to a professional is warranted.

3. They have difficulty coordinating gross, fine, or oral movements needed to produce more sophisticated gestures, signs, or speech.

Some children with certain disorders or syndromes like childhood apraxia of speech, cerebral palsy, or autism, and those with vision and auditory impairments and learning disabilities, may have difficulty coordinating, controlling, and executing the movements required for speech and signing. Approximations of a word (e.g., "ba" for *ball*) or a sign (e.g., tapping fists together for "more" instead of fingertips) should be encouraged and accepted. Alternative means of communication can also be introduced to establish functional communication.

Common First Words

This is a list of common first words adapted from *The Rossetti Infant Toddler Language Scale* (2006) and from the research findings of Professor Leslie Altman Rescorla, the director of the Child Study Institute at Bryn Mawr College.

ADJECTIVES *(Describing Words)*
- ☐ Big
- ☐ Cold
- ☐ Dirty
- ☐ Hot
- ☐ Little
- ☐ Old
- ☐ Thirsty
- ☐ Tired
- ☐ Wet
- ☐ Yucky

EARLY PRONOUNS
- ☐ I
- ☐ Me
- ☐ Mine
- ☐ You

PREPOSITIONS *(or Early Location Words)*
- ☐ Down
- ☐ Here
- ☐ In
- ☐ On
- ☐ Out
- ☐ There
- ☐ Up

NOUNS *(Person, Place, or Thing)*
- ☐ Apple
- ☐ Arms
- ☐ Baby
- ☐ Ball
- ☐ Balloon
- ☐ Banana
- ☐ Bath
- ☐ Bear/Teddy
- ☐ Belly/Tummy
- ☐ Bike
- ☐ Bird
- ☐ Book
- ☐ Boots
- ☐ Boy
- ☐ Bug
- ☐ Bunny
- ☐ Candy
- ☐ Car
- ☐ Cat/ Kitty
- ☐ Chair
- ☐ Cheese
- ☐ Choo-Choo
- ☐ Church
- ☐ Clock
- ☐ Coat
- ☐ Comb
- ☐ Cookie
- ☐ Cracker
- ☐ Cup
- ☐ Dada/ Daddy
- ☐ Diaper
- ☐ Dog/ Doggie
- ☐ Drink
- ☐ Ears
- ☐ Eyes
- ☐ Feet
- ☐ Fingers
- ☐ Flowers
- ☐ Girl
- ☐ Grandma
- ☐ Grandpa
- ☐ Gum
- ☐ Hair
- ☐ Hands
- ☐ Hat
- ☐ Horse/ Horsey
- ☐ Hot Dog
- ☐ Juice
- ☐ Key
- ☐ Legs
- ☐ Mama/ Mommy
- ☐ Milk
- ☐ Mouth
- ☐ Nose
- ☐ Paper
- ☐ Phone
- ☐ Pizza
- ☐ Potty
- ☐ Purse
- ☐ Rock
- ☐ Shirt
- ☐ Shoe
- ☐ Sky
- ☐ Sleep
- ☐ Snow
- ☐ Sock
- ☐ Spoon
- ☐ Stick
- ☐ Stove
- ☐ Teeth
- ☐ Toes
- ☐ Toy
- ☐ Truck
- ☐ TV

SOCIAL WORDS
- ☐ Bye
- ☐ Hi/Hello
- ☐ Huh?
- ☐ More
- ☐ Shhh
- ☐ Thank you
- ☐ Uh-oh
- ☐ What?
- ☐ What's that?
- ☐ Yes/Yeah

VERBS *(Action Words)*
- ☐ Comb
- ☐ Done
- ☐ Drink
- ☐ Eat
- ☐ Fall
- ☐ Go
- ☐ Go bed
- ☐ Go bye-bye
- ☐ Go night-night
- ☐ Go Out
- ☐ Put
- ☐ See
- ☐ Sit
- ☐ Sleep
- ☐ Snow
- ☐ Swing
- ☐ Want

ADDITIONAL TYPES
(These may include Quantity, Animal Sounds, and Rejection)
- ☐ All (all gone)
- ☐ Done (all done)
- ☐ Moo
- ☐ Don't
- ☐ Neigh-neigh
- ☐ No
- ☐ Quack-quack

Scanlon
Speech Therapy

Common First Words

O N THE PREVIOUS page, you will see a list of commonly spoken first words. This word list is important for two reasons.

1. The list shares insight into what words most two-year-old children commonly produce.

As you'll see, the majority of these words are pretty tangible, straightforward, and fairly easy to say. Typically, the first fifty words children say are ones that refer to objects or familiar people they can play with, manipulate, or use (Roseberry-McKibbin & Hedge, 2006). These often include the names of family members, toys, animals, and vehicles (i.e. nouns). Nouns are easier for young children to learn for two main reasons. First, parents are more likely to label what the child is playing with, looking at, or wanting, and this makes it easier for children to link the name to the item. Secondly, early nouns are more concrete and easier to identify than action words. Toddlers often look at the thing being labeled and then back at the person who is labeling it, further reinforcing their understanding.

Action words or verbs, and describing words or adjectives, on the other hand, often emerge later and are a bit more challenging to acquire. Actions are more fleeting and abstract in nature, making them potentially harder to identify and recognize. Understanding and applying the correct usage of verbs is also much more involved. Adjectives, too, are complex in nature. Since adjectives are words that describe or modify nouns, the child has to first understand the concept and then link that concept to a word. This may sound easy, but it is quite difficult because the toddler has to know that the adjective is describing a single characteristic and not the whole item. Therefore, the toddler has to attend to the word and try to pinpoint its meaning by zeroing in on the property being described (Sandhofer & Smith, 2007).

Attempting to explain all the intricacies of verb and adjective learning is not needed for our purposes. You only need to know a general gist about early verb and adjective development and recognize the importance of both, particularly verbs in future language expansion.

Despite the fact that verbs and adjectives usually emerge after nouns, it appears that some verbs and adjectives do emerge in early vocabularies. Once again, look at the "Common First Words" on page 27. So why do these words seem to emerge early even though verbs and adjectives are later developing? This probably happens because these verbs and adjectives make sense to the toddler and are relevant to his world. For instance, young toddlers love to put objects into one another, dump them out, and do it all over again. The earliest verbs to emerge are ones that are not true verbs but act like verbs because they accompany an action. Thus, if your toddler was playing in such a way and saying, "In," "Out," "Up," or "Down," while technically not verbs, these words would be considered early verbs because of the actions being performed by the child. Furthermore, as mentioned before, toddlers tend to say words that they understand. A toddler playing with blocks and putting them in and out of a box or container is performing the action of putting something in and then taking it out. So he has some idea of what *in* and *out* mean.

Toddlers then progress to using general, all-purpose verbs like *go, make,* and *do* because they are nonspecific in nature and can be used to describe many situations. Keep this in mind when choosing target words for your child. It is fine to model and use more descriptive, specific words around your toddler because we want to provide a rich language environment, but I wouldn't expect your little one to say a word like *depart* before saying the word *go.*

Objects too big for toddlers to manipulate are rarely first words (Tardif et al., 2008). To encourage first words, particularly early verbs, we should thoughtfully ponder what the toddler is thinking while he or she is manipulating or interacting with certain objects or people. Being mindful about this information will guide you to select words to target.

In the early stages of language acquisition, it is important to use and introduce age-appropriate vocabulary, especially if there is a suspected delay. This is because the children will have a better chance of understanding, retaining, and trying to say the word. Dr. Janice Light and Dr. Kathryn Drager, speech-language pathologists and professors in the Department of Communication Sciences and Disorders at Pennsylvania State University, also believe young children should be introduced to the type of vocabulary they can appropriately use. "Kids should sound like kids. Kids use different words than adults do. Kids use different sentence structures than adults do." These are often single words and short phrases (Light & Drager, n.d.). Researchers from the University of Edinburgh even found that eighteen-month-olds were more inclined to say, "Choo-choo," or "Night-night," as opposed to "train" or "goodnight," because it was easier for them to understand and say the names of objects with repeated syllables rather than words with nonidentical syllables (University of Edinburgh, 2016). Another observation is that many common first words are monosyllabic, start and end with a consonant, and have a vowel in the middle (e.g., "coat" or "hot"). In the speech-therapy circle, these are known as CVC (consonant-vowel-consonant) words. Other commonly spoken first words, that have more than one syllable, often end with an "ee" sound, like "cookie," "potty," "bunny," and "Daddy." This is known as *diminutization*, and it is a common speech pattern for toddlers.

Despite young children's propensity for acquiring seemingly simple first words, this does not mean they should be limited in their exposure to new, varied, and robust vocabulary. This is especially true once children have acquired what is known as a core vocabulary. A core vocabulary consists of a set of words that are used frequently across many settings and contexts.

Furthermore, basic, age-appropriate verbs should be introduced early on, even though verbs are later developing, because they are more challenging to acquire, especially for toddlers who may have a language delay.

2. The list can help you determine what words your toddler is saying or what words are missing from your toddler's inventory.

Without having a frame of reference, sometimes it's tricky to know exactly what words your child says, or should be saying, or what words he is not saying. Viewing this list may provide some support and a context. Maybe it made you realize that your son is saying much more than you initially thought. Or maybe it helped you to recognize that even though Joshua doesn't say many nouns, he says several social words. Or maybe it made you aware that Andy only says an assortment of nouns, along with the words "No," "Down," and "Up" but doesn't say *any* verbs. As mentioned before, verbs are powerful in regulating a toddler's environment and driving word combinations. If you notice a category of words completely missing from your toddler's repertoire, particularly verbs, it is wise to target them. If you're looking at this list with panic, thinking, "Oh no, Maria, is twenty-three months old and only saying four words from this list!" If this is the case, continue reading, as your loving involvement during this critical period of language growth is vital to your child's progress.

I hope part one answered some of your questions and provided enough background information on early language development to move us into part two.

Question from a Parent

I realize my daughter, Pilar, is not speaking nearly as much as her peers, but how many words should she actually be saying now?

—Father of Pilar, a twenty-seven-month-old

VOCABULARY DEVELOPS VERY quickly in the first few years of life. As a result, there is a wide range of what is considered typical, and the achievement of these early communication milestones may vary. Regardless, though, there is a predictable progression for language acquisition. Table 3 provides general ranges on vocabulary milestones and shows what is expected at various ages:

TABLE 3: Early Vocabulary Development

AGE	APPROXIMATE WORDS IN EXPRESSIVE VOCABULARY
Twelve months	Two to six words First words emerge between nine and fifteen months. "Mama" and "Dada" are universally the most common first words.
Fifteen months	Ten words
Eighteen to Nineteen months	Fifty words At this stage, children begin to put together simple telegraphic word combinations, such as "Daddy cup" or "Daddy drop cup."
Twenty-four months	Two hundred to three hundred words At twenty-one months, children have between twenty-six and twenty-nine verbs.

AGE	APPROXIMATE WORDS IN EXPRESSIVE VOCABULARY
Thirty months	Four hundred and fifty words At thirty months, children have between eighty-one and eighty-seven verbs.
Thirty-six months	One thousand words At this stage, children are asking questions and talking about past events.
Forty-two months	Twelve hundred words
Forty-eight months	Sixteen hundred words At this stage, children are using language to express their ideas and feelings, answering various questions like "Who?" "Why?" "Where?" "How?" and "When?"; beginning to tell simple, short stories, and engaging in basic conversation with others.

Adapted from: Language Development in Children, n.d; Lanza & Flahive, 2012; The Florida State University College of Medicine, n.d; Hadley et al., 2016; & Nelson, 1973.

Analyze Your Toddler's Language

Now, it is time to *informally* analyze your toddler's language skills. Notice I used the word *informally*. Your thoughtful efforts in this part will not replace a formal speech and language evaluation. The purpose of *My Toddler's First Words* is to guide your personal, and perhaps private, efforts in facilitating your toddler's early language development. Think of part two as an exercise in improving your awareness and ability to observe what your child does and does not do. Your efforts here will also guide you to complete the workbook portion in part four.

Complete the following four worksheets:

1 Words My Toddler Says

➤ Take inventory of your toddler's words or word approximations.

2 Words My Toddler Does Not Say

➤ Record words missing from your toddler's inventory of words.

3 Important and Special Words to Target

➤ Make a list of motivating words to target.

➤ These can be words that are important to your toddler and words that are important to your family.

4 Initial Words to Target

➤ Create a list of initial words to target by combining the words from the worksheet "Words My Toddler Does Not Say" and the motivating words from the worksheet "Important and Special Words to Target."

To complete worksheets one and two, observe your toddler a few moments throughout the day. Perform your observation in an environment that is familiar and comfortable to your toddler. Watch your toddler participating in a daily routine, like taking a bath. Or, observe him playing with some of his favorite toys. What words does he independently say? Do any of the words properly constitute the definition of a word? Record any words or word approximations on the worksheet, "Words My Toddler Says" on page 36. If your child is consistently using certain signs in a sign language (e.g., like the sign *eat* or *water*) you may also record that with a caveat that she is signing the word but not saying it yet.

While you are observing, you may also notice what your child is *not* saying. What words do you think your child should say to communicate more effectively? These words may be functional (requesting or rejecting words), or they may be fun (silly sounds and interjections). Record these missing words on the worksheet, "Words My Toddler Does Not Say" on page 40.

There will be times when you are not 100 percent sure of what to record; "What word did my child just say?" Was it a word?" or even, "I have no idea what he wants or is trying to tell me." This is okay. You're observing a complex little individual who is bursting with wonder, impulsivity, and unpredictability. If your toddler is not yet talking or only using a few spoken words, we often have to assume their needs and wants. These assumptions should be based on prior experiences with your toddler, what you already know about your special toddler, and the context. As already stated, one of the most important aspects in completing these worksheets is to increase your ability to observe how your toddler communicates. When you are not too sure what your toddler said or why he is screaming "Duh, duh", enlist the help of another person who knows your toddler and can aid you in interpreting the situation.

Words My Toddler Says

O N THE FOLLOWING page, you will find a worksheet to complete. Use this worksheet to record any words or word approximations your toddler says independently and with no support or prompting.

There are four columns to complete. Columns three and four require some thought and are optional to complete. If you have concerns regarding the diversity of your toddler's vocabulary or his or her social communication skills, I highly recommend completing these columns.

1   In the first column, record the word or word approximation (e.g., "pweez") spoken by your toddler.

2   In the second column, record the intended target word (e.g., "please").

3   In the third column, record the type of word produced.

A *word approximation* is a simplified version of the target word. For example, a child may say, "Dah," for dog. This can commonly occur with young children because they are learning how to say sounds and how to combine sounds together.

4   In the fourth column, record your toddler's communicative purpose for saying that word. For instance, he may say "pweez" when he is requesting something. As mentioned previously, sometimes your toddler's communicative purposes will not be obvious. During these times, embrace the ambiguity and try to decipher his intentions based on what you know about your toddler and the context.

Words My Toddler Says

Date_____

As of the above date, my toddler currently says the following words or word approximations independently and with no support or prompting from myself:

TODDLER'S WORD PRODUCTION	TODDLER'S INTENDED WORD	TYPE OF WORD	COMMUNICATIVE FUNCTION*
e.g. "Caw"	Car	Noun	To comment
e.g. "Eee"	Eat	Verb	To request

*Types of Communication Functions

Request, Reject or protest, Label, Comment, Ask questions, or Socially interact

Please do not feel discouraged if there are a lot of blanks in the table. With some effort and support, your toddler's language will blossom.

THIS PAGE IS REPRODUCIBLE AND DOWNLOADABLE AT MYTODDLERTALKS.COM

A Note on Bilingual Language Development

IF YOUR TODDLER is learning two languages, it is best to count the total words in his vocabulary. This means taking the sum of the words spoken across both languages. Counting the total number of words spoken in both languages is one of the best ways to gauge a toddler's language at this stage. This is because the vocabulary knowledge of a child learning two languages is distributed across the two languages (Core, Hoff, Rumiche & Senor, 2013). It is not fair or accurate to count words in only one language. Parents of children, who are learning more than one language, often have many questions about language development. Please know that bilingualism does not cause language delay. In truth, there are many cognitive advantages to being bilingual.

Words My Toddler Does Not Say

DURING THOSE MOMENTS of observing your toddler, did you notice any instances when he should have uttered a word but didn't?

- Maybe he needed help taking his shoe off, but he only grunted or gestured to you instead of saying, "Shoe," or "Off."

- Maybe he wanted another cookie but only pointed or tried to grab another from the countertop instead of saying, "Cookie," or "More."

- Maybe he didn't say anything, not even "uh-oh," when his tower of blocks came crashing down.

What could your toddler have said to more effectively communicate his or her needs, wants, interests, feelings, or initial reactions?

If you are struggling to notice what words are missing from your toddler's inventory, I suggest observing other children of your child's age. What words are they saying, or how are they communicating? How is their level of communication different from your child's? You can also look through the list of words on the "Common First Words List" (on page 27) to notice words that may be missing. In addition, do not be afraid to ask the opinion of another family member, caregiver, or daycare provider. He or she may offer further insight and information. These contemplative exercises will guide you to thoughtfully observe how your toddler communicates and see where the communication may breakdown.

Words My Toddler Does Not Say

COMMUNICATION INTENTION (What did your toddler want?)	COMMUNICATION ACTION OR SOUND (Did your toddler grab your hand and lead you to something? Did he look at you expectantly? Did he wait for you to get what he needed or wanted?)	WORD THAT SHOULD HAVE BEEN SPOKEN (He should have said "help" or "more" or "off.")
He wanted to open the door.	He looked at me and yelled bloody murder as he tried to pull the door open.	He should have said "Open."

Friendly Reminder

ANY PRELINGUISTIC BEHAVIORS*[3] that are unacceptable (e.g., screaming, yelling, hitting, shoving objects away), or difficult to understand and interpret, should be replaced with a target word. Replacement is recommended because continuing to rely on these behaviors is limiting and may result in increased communication breakdowns and frustration (Sigafoos et al., 2004).

---

3 Prelinguistic behaviors are behaviors or actions such as eye gaze, gestures, body movements, and vocalizations that individuals use before knowing how to use words to communicate. If the prelinguistic behavior is intentional, it can be meaningful and have purpose (e.g., Mary is looking and pointing to the cookie, so this must mean that she wants it), but it is not yet symbolic. This is because words and sign language are symbols, representing something else, but behaviors are not. Behaviors have to be interpreted.

Words That Are Important to My Toddler and Special to Our Family

TODDLERS ARE HIGHLY motivated by what they need, want, and like. Therefore, they'll want to know and use words that help them achieve their goals and desires. Toddlers' personalities also dictate what types of words they will try to say. Some toddlers are silly and have a sense of humor, while others are more shy or serious. If we target motivating words, toddlers realize language is fun, functional, and rewarding all at the same time! This understanding makes them more likely to communicate because doing so causes a reaction from others. Also, what a toddler hears strongly influences what he or she says. If there are words that are regularly spoken in your household, these could be highly motivating for your toddler to learn too.

Generate a list of motivating words.

Consider your toddler's favorite foods, places, and toys as well as expressions that he or she may find silly. Contemplate your family's dynamic, culture, or traditions. Are there any unique or special words you would like your toddler to say? For instance, if your toddler is close to his grandma, calling her "Nana," "Grammy," or "Nonna" would be heartwarming to hear. If your toddler loves Mickey Mouse or Curious George or eating cheese or apples, or if he or she enjoys playing a game of chase or tickle, knowing how to say these words is important and highly motivating. While you are creating this list, you may notice that some of the words from "Words My Toddler Does Not Say" are also here. This overlap is expected.

Select a variety of types of words (e.g., nouns, adjectives, verbs) and choose words that can serve different communicative functions.

Important and Special Words to Target

POTENTIAL TARGET WORD	TYPE OF WORD	COMMUNICATIVE FUNCTION*
Ball	*Noun*	*To comment and share enjoyment*

*Types of Communication Functions

Request, Reject or protest, Label, Comment, Ask questions, or Socially interact

Do you think these words are easy to say? If a word contains many syllables or has later developing sounds (e.g., "sh," "s," "th," "r," "z," and "l") and your child is not yet saying these sounds, then this word may be harder for your child to initially imitate or repeat. For instance, if your child likes Curious George, it may be easier for him to say "George," "Georgie," or an approximation of George, before expecting him to say "Curious George."

Circle the words you think would be easy for your child to say.

Brainstorming Ideas

➤ "Every time Rocco is thirsty, he insists on drinking from the same superhero cup and only wants that cup. It would be nice if he could somehow tell me that he wants the Batman cup or 'bat cup.'"

➤ "It would be great if Greg could tell me that he wants a snack by saying, 'Eat' or 'Num num' instead of climbing on the counter and rummaging through the cabinets."

➤ "I would love it if Victoria could say, 'Open,' to avoid a complete meltdown."

➤ "Aidan sees his grandmother several times a week. It would be nice if he could say, 'Nonna,' when he sees her."

➤ "We would love if Axel could say, 'Amen,' after we say grace at dinnertime."

➤ "Jayden likes to watch basketball with his daddy. It would be awesome if he could try to say part or all of the expression 'raise the roof' when his team scores a point."

Master List of Initial Words to Target

Now you will create a master list of initial words to target. Take the words you recorded in "Words My Toddler Does Not Say" and "Words That Are Important to My Toddler and Special to Our Family," and log them onto this list. Target these words by using the techniques and suggestions from part three and by completing the 30-day workbook in part four of *My Toddler's First Words.*

POTENTIAL TARGET WORD	TYPE OF WORD	COMMUNICATIVE FUNCTION*
Bye	*Social Word*	*Socially interact*

*Types of Communication Functions

Request, Reject or protest, Label, Comment, Ask questions, or Socially interact

THIS PAGE IS REPRODUCIBLE AND DOWNLOADABLE AT MYTODDLERTALKS.COM

Get Your Toddler Talking

Techniques to Elicit First Words

LANGUAGE LEARNING SHOULD be a natural and fun process. It should not be highly structured, fabricated, or inauthentic. Research supports that the best way to encourage first words is by using naturalistic intervention strategies (University Center for Excellence in Developmental Disabilities Education, Research, and Service, n.d. & Woods et al., 2011). The marketing of educational products like first-words flash cards can be persuasive. It's not unusual to meet parents or caregivers who think if they make their children sit down and view flash cards, they will acquire new words and start saying them. No matter how touchy-feely, pretty, or big the flash cards, they do not replace naturalistic intervention strategies. Drilling your toddler with flashcards is not a natural way for her to learn language. Naturalistic teaching strategies should occur frequently, and there should be multiple exposures and opportunities to use and practice language and new words.

Eight Naturalistic Language Strategies to Increase Early Language Development

1 Identify and appreciate the child's lead.

2 Be responsive.

3 Pause in anticipation.

4 Set it up.

5 Give choices.

6 Imitate, imitate, imitate.

7 Create predictable play routines.

8 Strategically prompt for target words.

In this section, I explain each strategy by providing an easy-to-understand definition, followed by examples of the technique in action. What-not-to-do examples are also provided. These examples are not meant to be critical of your efforts. They illustrate what I sometimes see from well-intentioned parents and caregivers. I want you to avoid such frustrating roadblocks and be more efficient with your time.

1. Identify and appreciate the child's lead.

What is this?

Identifying and appreciating the child's lead consists of following his attention and interest. Talk about the thing, person, or event that is capturing your child's attention. If he is touching a toy truck, talk about the truck; if she is looking at a dog, talk about the dog. Acknowledge his words, phrases, and actions by saying and doing something related to his interest. Model or copy his actions, and then repeat what he attempts to say.

Adults who are particularly skilled in using this technique are present in the moment, observant, and sensitive to reading and responding to a child's behaviors and actions. According to a research synthesis by Dr. Carl Dunst and Dr. Carol Trivette, researchers at Orelena Hawks Puckett Institute, "A caregiver's ability to read and respond to the child's behaviors accurately and promptly supports a child's initiation of communication and encourages continued interaction through reinforcement of the child's behavior and the success of the interaction" (Woods et al., 2011, p. 383).

An example of identifying and appreciating the child's lead

It is a sunny spring morning, and you notice your toddler is looking out the window while you are sitting on the couch, drinking coffee. Suddenly, two birds fly out of a tree and stop at the bird feeder in the backyard. Your toddler is fascinated and points to the birds and smiles at you. You identify and appreciate your toddler's attention and interest by saying, "You see the birds?" while pointing to the two birds. "Those birds are hungry. They are eating the birdseed." Talk about those birds and describe what they are doing.

What is it not?

Many speech-language pathologists who are familiar with this technique probably know it as "following the child's lead." In fact, in *My Toddler Talks*, I referred to this technique by that term. However, this term can be misinterpreted to mean that the child should dictate everything, leading to a free-for-all. Haphazardly jumping around from topic to topic or toy to toy is not

> Actually, the problem was more her methods were a bit too chaotic. Her office has toys everywhere, and she encourages George to jump from one thing to the next and never really got him to focus. It was kind of stressful.
>
> —Mom of George,
> a twenty-four-month-old,
> regarding a prior speech-therapy session

beneficial. There's no learning in chaos. If you are playing or interacting with a toddler, and he is getting very distracted, and you feel like you are aimlessly bouncing around the room, then things are probably too chaotic. Toddlers do not have long attention spans. But when they are interested in something, they can attend to it longer. Appreciating a child's lead enables us to extend the attention span by recognizing her interests and then expanding upon those interests. If chaos is occurring, perhaps it is because you haven't found something engaging enough for your toddler. Or the environment is too distracting. Are too many toys out in the open? Consider limiting the number of toys, and therefore distractions, by taking out only one or two at a time. Rotating your child's toys on a monthly or seasonal basis is also advisable so they continually seem fresh and new.

An example of identifying and appreciating the child's lead gone awry
You see the birds and say, "Oh yeah, two bluebirds. How nice! What should we do today?" In this case, you acknowledged your child's attention and interest but then quickly changed the subject.

As sensitive adults who want to support our children's learning, we need to support their thinking by expanding upon their interests. Do this by selectively reinforcing appropriate interests. Luke Touhill (n.d.), an early-childhood consultant and writer, expresses the following about how we should use children's interests to promote learning:

When considering the balance between adult and child direction, it can help if we think about *using* children's interests rather just *following* them. When we see ourselves as following children's interests we tend to see children as being in charge of the program, which may lead us to minimize our own role. If, however, we *use* children's interests, then we can see the interest as the starting point for what we do, rather than as the end point. It then becomes our role, in partnership with children, to convert the interest into an effective learning experience, rather than assuming an experience will be worthwhile simply because it is child-chosen or child-directed. (p. 1)

Why identify and appreciate the child's lead?

Identifying and appreciating the child's lead, as opposed to making the child do what we want him to do, ensures the experience is relevant and meaningful. Additionally, research has shown that a child's behavior is more positive when his learning is interest-based. This is particularly true for children with autism (Dunst, Trivette & Hamby, 2012). Learning is much easier and more effective when the learner is attentive, present, and engaged.

When should we identify and appreciate the child's lead?

Identifying and appreciating a child's lead is usually a very good place to start most speech-therapy sessions. It is particularly important to do when working with a child who struggles to attend or cooperate or who has limited interests.

> Children can only be interested in what they already know about. If our focus is only on what children are already interested in, we will have a limited pool of ideas and interests to draw on.
>
> —Luke Touhill, n.d., p. 2

2. Be responsive.

What is this?

Being responsive consists of quickly responding to our child's focus of attention or any of her attempts to communicate. These communication attempts may be verbal (a word or a word attempt) or nonverbal (a gesture or a gaze). Respond quickly, almost immediately, to these communication attempts. If you suspect your child may have autism, experts recommend responding within three seconds (Haebig, McDuffie, & Weismer, 2013). This way, she has a better chance of connecting what she is thinking about to the word you have provided.

An example of being responsive to the child's focus of attention

While you are washing the dishes, you notice that Mason is staring intently at a huge cricket that has somehow gotten into the house. Mason points to the cricket. Now you are both looking at and focused on the cricket, and you say, "Cricket. That's a huge cricket."

An example of being responsive to verbal and nonverbal communication attempts

Sam tries to retrieve the bottle of bubbles from the shelf but needs your assistance. So he comes up to you and points to the bubbles. You respond immediately by saying, "Bubbles? You want the bubbles?" By doing so, you are responding quickly and naturally rewarding Sam by giving him the desired object and by saying its name. Sam will quickly realize that words are powerful and can be used to attain desired items or meet his needs and wants.

If Sam tries to say bubbles—"Buhbuh"—you can immediately respond by repeating his verbal attempt, "Bubbles," and then giving them to him. You can also be responsive by expanding upon or adding to what

your child says. In the case of the bubbles, you may say, "Bubbles? Blow bubbles? Do you want to blow bubbles?" Expansions are good for promoting later language growth.

What is it not?

Being responsive is not diverting your child's attention to something or someone else. Making a noncontingent comment or saying something unrelated to what your child is focused on, will not necessarily support his communication. It also does not involve asking too many questions or placing too many demands on getting your child to speak. Once you start asking many questions or try to direct an action, you are no longer responding or reacting to your toddler's communication attempt. Rather, you are directing the communication.

An example of not being responsive to the child's focus of attention

Ava is playing with her favorite doll, Sally. She is feeding Sally the play food you just purchased at the local toy store. You are thrilled that Ava really seems to enjoy playing with this recent purchase. Ava picks up a pretend artichoke and curiously looks at it. With excitement and gusto, you join in on the play, pick up a banana, and say, "Here's a banana, Ava. Give it to Sally." In this example, it's fantastic that you're playing and talking with Ava. But you may have missed an opportunity to name this new and interesting food—"artichoke."

An example of not being responsive to verbal and nonverbal communication attempts

While feeding her doll, Sally, more pretend food, Ava picks up the cucumber, shows it to you, and says,

"Cuhcum," attempting to say, "Cucumber." You get so excited with Ava's attempt to say cucumber that you whip out your phone to shoot a quick video of Ava saying cucumber again – her grandparents would love to see this! You pick up the cucumber, point to it and say, "Ava, what is this?" Ava does not respond. You try again, "Ava, sweetie what is it?" She stares at you. You say, "Ava, you said it before. Say it again. It's a cucumber. Say cucumber for nana and pop." Ava grabs the cucumber out of your hand and walks away. In this example, you were so overcome with joy that you forgot to respond to her attempt to say cucumber. Replying, "Cucumber! Yes, that's a cucumber" would have been responsive. Asking her to perform and to say it again is not responsive. This is more like directing a cast member in a movie.

Why be responsive?

Responding quickly and contingently promotes the learning of new words because providing labels for what the child is focused on helps her directly map the new word to the object or activity of his or her attention (Haebig, McDuffie & Weismer, 2013). When you comment on what your child is focusing on (e.g., the cricket and the artichoke), there is no expectation she will imitate you. You're doing this to expose your child to new vocabulary so she can correctly map the new word to what she sees, feels, or touches.

> A contingent response is when the quality, intensity, and timing of the other's signals clearly reflect the signals that we have sent. With contingent interpersonal interactions, we create a neural sense of grounding and empowerment in a social world of connections. These kinds of connections create a strong, internal coherence of the self.
>
> —Dr. Dan Siegal,
> neuropsychiatrist and author

3. Pause in anticipation.

What is this?

Pausing in anticipation is when you wait approximately five seconds (count inwardly three to five Mississippis) to give your child a chance to respond to what you have asked, said, or done. While you are doing this, show that you are waiting for your toddler's response by raising your eyebrows, smiling, and opening your mouth. Give your toddler cues that you are very excited and interested in what he may say or do.

An example of pausing in anticipation

You and your toddler walk into a room, and immediately, your toddler's eyes light up as he sees five big balloons in the corner. You identify and appreciate his lead and point to the balloons with your eyes raised and your mouth open.

Pause in anticipation, remembering to count three to five Mississippis, to see what the child does. Maybe he'll copy your gesture and point to the balloons, copy your facial expression, or try to say something.

Next, you can say, "Wow, look at those balloons!"

Pause in anticipation. Wait to see what the child does or says. This time, you provided a few target words for him to potentially imitate ("wow," "look," or "balloons"), if he so chooses.

The end goal is that your child will perform an action or gesture or say something.

What is it not?

Pausing in anticipation is not prompting for a certain word or phrase. There should be no direct pressure for the child to respond a certain way.

An example of pausing in anticipation gone awry

When the caregiver sees the balloons, she immediately says, "Oh, Charlie, look at those balloons. How cool! There are five balloons. There's a red balloon, a blue balloon, a yellow balloon, a green balloon, and an orange balloon. You know the word *balloon*." She quickly looks at Charlie, and says, "Can you say 'balloon'? Without waiting for Charlie to respond and without giving her a chance to say anything, the caregiver utters, say 'balloon.'"

In this example, the caregiver bombarded the child with the word *balloon*. It is okay to repeat and bombard your child with target words but this goodhearted person did *not* give the child a chance to initiate or spontaneously say anything. In fact, she wanted the toddler to specifically say, "Balloon" at that exact moment. Imagine being the child. How do you think Charlie felt in this situation?

Why pause in anticipation?

Pausing in anticipation gives your child the power to decide how and when he wants to communicate. This may be with a look, a pull, a point, a reach, a sound, a word, or even a phrase. It also gives your child the chance to process the information and allows him the opportunity to become an active communicator. Doing so encourages spontaneous, natural communication. Not requiring your child to say something specific, increases the likelihood that he will initiate communication. This will help him to realize the need to communicate to get what he wants. If you are always anticipating your child's needs and wants or prompting—"Say, 'more,'" "Say, 'Truck,'" or "Say, 'Ball'"—the child may become reliant or dependent on the prompt. This is especially the case for children with autism.

When should we pause in anticipation?

Pausing in anticipation is an excellent technique to use with all children but especially with those who are passive communicators. Passive communicators are those who usually do not initiate comments or questions but rather imitate or echo words. Pausing allows the child time to process what is said and freely respond.

4. Set it up.

What is this?

Setting it up entails designing a scenario that encourages communication. We create temptations to motivate children to talk. In the speech-therapy circle, this is known as environmental arrangement. We provide opportunities for communication by manipulating the environment. Position favorite toys or desired objects in sight but out of reach. Play with a toy that is broken and needs to be fixed or play with a toy that is missing a functional piece such as a car without a wheel. Give your child a task you know he may struggle with, such as opening a sealed transparent bag with toys inside. Setting it up creates a motivating scenario that drives the child to ask for assistance.

An example of setting it up

Every morning since Christmas, Larry wakes up and immediately wants to play with his new fire truck. Instead of instantly giving it to him, you opt to elicit some communication. You position the fire truck,

on the kitchen counter top, where Larry can see it but cannot access it. Usually, the fire truck is on the floor in the family room. Putting his favorite toy on the counter top gives Larry the opportunity to point to the fire truck or to try to say it. If he cannot say it, that's OK. Provide a model like, "Fire truck?" Pause in anticipation. "You want the fire truck?" Pause. "Here's the fire truck." After attempting this strategy approximately two or three times, at the most, give Larry the fire truck. Your goal is not to force Larry to say the word nor is it to cause frustration. However, continue using the strategy of setting it up so that Larry is encouraged to communicate in other circumstances.

What is it not?

Sensitive caregivers and parents are very good at knowing what their children need and want, so they quickly meet their children's needs and wants. We take pride in knowing our children so well we can predict and anticipate their every whim. During the hustle and bustle of everyday life, it is easy to give our children everything they need or want before they even ask for it. But when we do this, we are eliminating an excellent opportunity to promote communication. Try not to over anticipate every need, want, and whim of your child. Set it up so your child has to communicate!

An example of not setting it up
Larry wakes up, runs into the living room, and begins frantically searching for his fire truck. Since you know the fire truck is in the basement, you quickly say, "Oh, you want your fire truck? I'll go get it."

Why set it up?
Setting it up aids the child in initiating communication. These temptations entice the child to interact and communicate.

When should we set it up?
You should set it up when you want your child to initiate more communication. Some children can be passive, and some are at risk of becoming prompt dependent.

5. Give choices.

What is this?
Giving choices is a more closed-ended way to ask your child a question about what she needs or wants.

Depending on the child, I like to give two choices at a time. Giving too many choices may increase confusion. The choices provided can be strategically manipulated to aid decision-making and language development.

- Pair a preferred choice with a nonpreferred choice. For example, you know your son hates green beans but loves peas, or he prefers Buzz Lightyear to Woody. You give him a choice between these two options because it is then easier for him to make a decision.
  → For instance, "Sammy, do you want to play with Woody or Buzz?"

- To encourage imitation, put the preferred choice last. The child will be more apt to remember the last thing you said, making it more likely that he will imitate you.
  → For instance, "Sammy, do you want to eat green beans (nonpreferred choice) or peas (preferred choice)?"

- To encourage processing, put the preferred object first. This works very well for children who tend to echo or always repeat the last thing you said without thinking about it.
  → For instance, "Sammy, do you want to eat peas (preferred choice) or green beans (non-preferred choice)?"

➤ Simultaneously say and show the choices if your child struggles to answer questions.

→ For instance, "Liam, do you want the truck or the car?" While saying, "Truck," pick up the truck with one hand (say it and show it), and while saying, "Car," pick up the car with the opposite hand (say it and show it).

What is it not?

Giving choices is not asking an open-ended question like, "What would you like to eat?" or "What should we do today?" These are great questions for encouraging social communication and reciprocity. But sometimes open-ended questions may be difficult for a language-delayed toddler to answer, especially if he has only a few sounds or words in his repertoire.

Why should we give choices?

When we give choices to toddlers, we tell them they have some control and their input matters. Providing choices also encourages decision-making and promotes language development. When we ask choice questions, we are providing models of the potential target words for the child to imitate. It is easier for the child to respond to a choice question versus an open-ended question like, "What do you want to play with?" because he hears "truck" and "airplane" in the choice question. Giving choices not only makes it easier for the child to potentially imitate and repeat, but it also allows the child to point or gesture if he can't say anything yet. For example, the child points to the airplane just like an adult at the restaurant points to a gentleman at the next table who is eating the *petits pâtés a la sage*. This adult points to the gentleman's plate because he either doesn't know the name of the man's meal or he needs to hear the name again before he can try to say it.

Giving choices also takes away the direct pressure of an open-ended question like, "Sammy, what should we play today?" Some children may have word-retrieval difficulties and may have difficulty remembering the name of something.

When should we give choices?

We can give choices when we feel the child has difficulty processing many different choices or when we want the child to imitate a specific target word.

6. Imitate, imitate, imitate.

What is it?

Imitation is the act of copying someone or something. Playwright George Bernard Shaw famously said, "Imitation is not just the sincerest form of flattery—it's the sincerest form of learning." The ability to imitate helps us to acquire new knowledge, socially communicate, and better understand something. We learn by watching others and trying to do what they do. Children who struggle to instinctively imitate gestures, body movements, sounds, or words have a much harder time acquiring speech and language. Research is emerging to show that intervention to enhance imitation skills can lead to an increase in sound and word production. Faculty from Texas Woman's University, used imitation therapy with five non-verbal eighteen to nineteen month old children during an eight to nine week period. They found that all five children demonstrated remarkable increases in both the number of vocalizations and the variety of sounds produced (Gill, Mehta, Fredenbury, & Bartlett, 2015). If your child appears to lack shared attention and doesn't readily imitate the gestures or sounds of others, then I highly recommend using this technique. Encouraging our children to imitate on the following three levels may promote the production of first words:

- ➤ Imitate actions with objects

- ➤ Imitate gestures or body movements

- ➤ Imitate sounds and words

First start by imitating your child. Begin by identifying and appreciating your child's lead then imitate what she is doing or saying. With the exception of crying or any negative actions like hitting or pushing, imitate everything your child does or says. If she picks up a block, you pick up another block. If she jumps up and down, you jump up and down. If she sighs or makes a sound while playing, you make the same exact sound. Whenever possible try to position yourself face-to-face with your child. We imitate and want our child to notice that we are imitating her because we aim to make her aware that she has the ability to influence and impact others (Gill, Mehta, Fredenbury, & Bartlett, 2015). This is very powerful. Once children know that their actions can influence others, they become more attentive to others and more intentional in their acts and in turn, are more likely to imitate others. Once your child realizes that you are imitating her and she is showing delight in her ability to manipulate you, then it is time to gradually entice your child to imitate your actions, gestures, body movements, sounds, or words.

Imitate actions with objects

Encourage your child to imitate your actions with objects. Observe what he is already doing with an object or toy (identify and appreciate the child's lead), imitate what he is doing with the object, and then take it a step further by adding to the action.

Imitate gestures or body movements

Encourage your child to imitate your gestures or body movements. Observe what she is already doing (identify and appreciate the child's lead). Next, imitate your child's gestures and body movements (she will love it!), and then take it a step further by adding to the gesture or body movement to encourage imitation.

Imitate sounds and words

Encourage your child to imitate your sounds or words. Start by observing what he is already engaged in. Next, imitate the sounds or words your child says. Then take it a step further by adding to the sound or word.

Examples

Imitate actions with objects. Maurice is quietly observing his daughter, Jasmin, play with a large set of stacking blocks. They are one of her favorite toys. He notices how she repeatedly takes a block and places it next to another one. The order is always the same, and the letters on the blocks are always with the letter side facing up. Maurice finishes his coffee, takes a handful of blocks from the bin, and quietly sits on the floor across from Jasmin. He begins by imitating her play. He picks up a block and lays one down, one after another. Jasmin looks up and notices her father is imitating her. They smile. Maurice continues this a few times. Then he decides to add to the play by stacking the blocks on top of one another instead of next to one another. When he finishes building a large tower of blocks, Jasmin looks up. While having Jasmin's attention, Maurice quickly knocks the tower over. They both smile and laugh. Maurice builds another tower. This time, he waits again for Jasmin to look up, and when she does, she knocks the tower over. Jasmin now takes the blocks and starts building her own tower to knock over again.

Imitate gestures or body movements. After being introduced to building towers and then knocking them down, Jasmin is now regularly building tall towers and knocking them down with her father. They are having a splendid time together. Maurice notices that Jasmin has started to clap her hands together after building each tower. So he starts clapping his hands too as a way to celebrate and share his joy. After clapping together for a few seconds, Maurice then begins to encourage Jasmin to give him a high five. Eventually, Jasmin not only starts to quickly respond to her father's requests for high fives but also then starts to initiate the high fives with him.

Imitate sounds and words. Jasmin's play with blocks is continuing to evolve. Maurice notices she is now trying to say more sounds and words. Just before she knocks down the tower, she seems to say something like "Ah" with an

open-mouth posture. So Maurice, now a big believer that imitation is key, imitates this sound and says, "Ah." He does this a few times and then adds to it by saying, "Ah...*boom!*" After a while, Jasmin begins to say, "Ah...*boo.*" She is deleting the final consonant, which is age appropriate for two years old.

What is it not?
An example of imitation gone awry

Martha noticed her son, Benjamin, rarely imitated any actions, gestures, or sounds. She was motivated to get him to talk, so she ran to the toy store and purchased some miniature cars and a car ramp. She showed Benjamin the toys, and his eyes lit up. She encouraged him to sit down at his table, took out the new toys, and told him, "Do and say what I do." Benjamin looked a little perplexed. Martha then said, "Do this," as she picked up a car and pushed it down the ramp. Instead, Benjamin picked up the car and spun its wheels. Martha ignored this and persisted in her plan. She repeated this drill-like activity about five times until Benjamin finally stood up and walked away from the table.

In this case, Martha forgot that the key is to imitate Benjamin first. Martha needs to create the awareness in Benjamin that what he does or says can influence another's attention and actions. Thus, she should have tried to imitate his action of spinning the wheels before making him push the cars down the ramp. If she had imitated his actions, it is more likely Benjamin would have been motivated to try to imitate Martha.

Why imitate?

Imitation is an essential step to acquiring speech and language skills. Children imitate as a way to understand another person's behavior (Marton & Gusztav, 2009). Imitation begins early in infancy. Babies imitate their caregiver's body movements, facial expressions, actions, and sounds. They imitate their caregivers not because they are told to imitate but because the back-and-forth exchange is enjoyable. The act of imitating is socially rewarding and engaging. This is how infants begin to learn about communication.

Before toddlers begin to spontaneously utter their first words, they usually imitate the sounds and words others say. And before they imitate your sounds and words, they imitate your actions and gestures.

When should we use imitation?

We should use imitation when we notice our children are lacking this vital skill.

7. Create predictable play routines.

What is it?

Making play predictable involves taking a child's favorite game, activity, or routine and infusing some structure, consistency, and turn taking into it. Doing something a child loves is most important, because we want the interaction to be enjoyable and intrinsically motivating.

If your child has a favorite activity, turn it into a play routine. I write extensively about this in *My Toddler Talks: Strategies and Activities to Promote Your Child's Language Development*. A play routine is a purposeful way of playing that follows a predictable sequence. It combines the excitement of play and the predictability of routine, thereby allowing for turn taking and multiple-language learning opportunities. The resulting framework of a play routine allows adults to bombard and expose children to targeted sounds and words while they are playing and having fun. The play routines in *My Toddler Talks* are a form of guided play. They are structured so toddlers can learn what to expect each time. The adult structures the routines, but the toddler is the one who makes the decisions and leads the way. The adult merely serves as a facilitator and guides the play to create and foster language learning. These routines are child-directed but with a purpose. This is because children learn to advance their play skills by interacting and playing with adults. These adults are usually their parents or caregivers.

> A play routine is a purposeful way of playing that follows a predictable sequence. It combines the excitement of play and the predictability of routine, thereby allowing for turn-taking and multiple language-learning opportunities.

Dr. Rachel E. White, a child psychologist and assistant professor of psychology at Hamilton College, explains that parents are fundamental players in the development of their children's play skills. In her article *The Power of Play: A Research Summary on Play and Learning*, White (n.d.) states,

> Early involvement from parents as initiators, directors, and partners in play serves to scaffold young children's abilities so that play structured by an adult is more sustained and sophisticated than the child would be able to achieve alone or with peers. As children mature, they begin to take initiative in generating their own activities but parents remain involved on the sidelines through comments and prompting. Play with parents sets the stage for children's ability to successfully play with peers. (p. 9)

Once a favorite activity is decided upon, observe how your child interacts and plays. Do you notice a pattern? Does the play or playful interaction follow a sequence? Usually, when a child enjoys an activity or game, he will repeat favorite parts, and sometimes a pattern or sequence will organically emerge. A primary distinction between free play and organized play, like Duck, Duck, Goose, is that in free play, children are free to do what they want to do, and they learn to create and adjust rules and form their own arrangements. Most play, regardless of whether it is free or structured, usually has a beginning, a middle, and an end. It starts a certain way (the beginning), and a chain of events follows (the middle), leading to a delightful end (the end).

If your child's play appears disorganized and disjointed, then it is your job to build some sequence, flow, and predictability into it. Doing so will help to organize and regulate your child's actions, increase his understanding, and eventually improve his language. Ensure there is predictability by creating intentional triggers in the play to prompt certain actions, sounds, or words from your child.

Encourage turn taking while playing, and guide your child to take a turn. To keep the motivation and turn taking going, I like to keep my turn (the adult's turn) short compared with the child's turn. When it is your turn, you can gently announce it's your turn: "Mommy's turn," "Daddy's turn," or "My turn." The child's turn does not necessarily require a verbal response. His turn can be making eye contact, gesturing to something, or handing you something.

An example of creating predictable play routines
Patrick watched his twenty-six-month-old son, Shane, play in his playroom. During this time, he noticed Shane went from toy to toy in a rather disorganized fashion. Shane seemed to get the most enjoyment from tearing apart his playroom. He picked up a toy, fussed with it for a little, and then discarded it shortly before moving on to another one. So Patrick took a shape sorter from the shelf and encouraged Shane to play with him. They sat on the floor across from each other. Patrick began the play by dropping a peg into a corresponding hole while saying, "In." After he finished his turn, he said, "Now, Shane's turn. It's your turn," while giving Shane the toy. Patrick allowed Shane to drop in a few pegs before announcing that it was his turn again—"Now, Daddy's turn. It's my turn"—while gently taking the shape sorter from Shane. This turn taking continued until Patrick noticed Shane's attention was starting to wane. So Patrick announced, "OK, last turn, Shane, and then we'll eat a snack!"

This example happens to be a naturally predictable play routine because Patrick and Shane are playing with a type of closed-ended toy. This toy has a clear end point. Therefore, it is easy to make the play predictable and to establish turn taking, making it a good choice for someone like Shane. Closed-ended toys are also good for building attention skills and promoting task completion. For more examples of closed-ended toys, please visit http://www.scanlonspeech. com/2014/05/25/7-close-ended-games-activities-and-toys-to-build-attention-in-preschoolers/.

Another example of creating predictable play routines

Every night before bed, Sarah and her mom, Grace, play a game called Tickle Mummy.*[4] Sarah loves this game. Over the course of playing it every night, Grace has noticed the game always starts the same way: She extends her arms like a mummy to try to catch and tickle Sarah while Sarah runs away from the Tickle Mummy. As Sarah runs away, she usually laughs and shakes her head no when the Tickle Mummy gets close.

---

4 If your child likes to be tickled for a few seconds or the anticipation of running away from a Tickle Mummy, then he or she may enjoy this play routine. If you child does not enjoy being tickled, then do something else.

Since Grace would like to encourage more words from Sarah, she has decided to create some triggers to encourage turn taking so Sarah can say something during these highly predictable moments. So as the Tickle Mummy gets close to Sarah, it asks, "Hmmm, should I tickle your belly or your feet?" (This refers to technique 5: give choices.) If Sarah responds with one of the choices, the Tickle Mummy obeys. If she does not respond, the Tickle Mummy chooses where it will tickle Sarah. After a few seconds of tickling, the Tickle Mummy lets Sarah run away again, and the pursuit continues. Each time the Tickle Mummy gets close to Sarah, it asks where it should tickle her (e.g., the belly, the feet, the arms). Eventually, Sarah begins to realize this is the Tickle Mummy's method of operation, and she learns to anticipate that she will have to respond.

This play continues until the Tickle Mummy gets tired. When this happens, it begins to slow down its movements and announces, "I'm getting sleepy." Sarah has learned this is how the play routine ends, so to make it more exciting, she has to cast a spell on the Tickle Mummy with her play wand. So the routine ends with Sarah casting a spell to put the Tickle Mummy to sleep, and sometimes Sarah even says, "Sleep." Tickle Mummy then peacefully goes to sleep.

What is it not?
Predictable play routines should not be boring.

When trying to infuse predictability and turn taking into play with your child, remember that the child has to think the play is fun, exciting, and inspiring. Once the child thinks it is work or boring, it ceases to be play. The adult has to keep this in mind when playing with a purpose.

An example of predictable play routines gone awry
Let's go back to the example of Patrick and Shane. Since Patrick had success playing with the shape sorter, he decided it would be a toy they could play with every day. So every morning after breakfast, Patrick would sit down with Shane, and they would play with the shape sorter. When Shane would start to disengage and try to escape to another room or select another toy, Patrick would say, "No, Shane, we have to work on your words using this toy." Approaching the play as work, Patrick forgot that variety is the spice of life; novelty and fun aids learning and memory (Fenker & Schutze, 2008). To keep things interesting, Patrick could have found other small, but safe toy objects that do not belong to the shape sorter and playfully tried to force them into the holes. Patrick could have made funny noises like, "grrrrr" while trying to unsuccessfully push the toys through the holes. This may have encouraged Shane to say something or to instruct his father to use the proper shapes. Either way, Shane may have been more attentive. If Patrick *did* introduce new ways to play with the shape sorter but Shane was still uninterested, perhaps it's time to introduce a different toy.

Why should we create predictable play routines?
Structuring predictability into play helps children initiate communication because they can anticipate what will happen next. The play becomes predictable enough to provide a framework for learning language

and increasing communication. When toddlers can anticipate what comes next, and if they like what's coming next, they will attend, engage, and participate. Effectively structured play can allow two things to happen that would not happen in a free-play situation: The adult can provide additional support to model or expose his or her child to new targeted vocabulary, and the adult can purposefully elicit certain words or responses, therefore increasing the opportunities for the child to respond or say a word (Eisenberg, 2004).

When should we create predictable play routines?
We should structure predictability and turn taking at various times:

➤ When we need to balance the turn taking so one person, often the adult or experienced communicator, is not dominating the activity or routine too much

➤ When the child appears to benefit from hearing repeated models of a word or target and needs to have multiple opportunities to practice producing a desired response

Once the child has grown accustomed to the predictable play routine and readily uses the language targets, the routine can then be altered or expanded to maintain the child's interest and further enhance language learning.

Question from a Parent

But what about making my child say the word? Sometimes I know that Molly can say the word "help" because she has said it a few times, but usually she resorts to handing me the item that she needs help with rather than saying the word. Should I make her say, "Help"?
—Parent of Molly, a twenty-month-old

SOMETIMES IT IS appropriate to gently prompt your child to say a word, especially if she can say the word to request something, someone, or some action. Technique 8 will address how to encourage production of a particular word.

8. Strategically prompt for target words.

What is it?

Prompting for words consists of naturalistic and conversation-based ways to increase expressive vocabulary in young children with general developmental delays (Fey, Yoder, Warren & Bredin-Oja, 2013; Kaiser, 2011).

There are four different ways to prompt your child to say a particular word, each differing in their levels of support. Please see table 4 below.

TABLE 4: **Prompts to Help Your Child Say a Target Word**

TYPE OF PROMPT	EXAMPLE	LEVEL OF SUPPORT
Use of a time delay (similar to pausing in anticipation)	Your child would like to eat peas and is grabbing for the bowl. You pause up to five seconds and wait expectantly for your child to say "peas" before handing him the bowl of peas.	The least amount of support since no language is being used
Open prompt	"What would you like to eat?" This is not a testing question. There is no correct response to the question. It is to encourage the child to make a request.	A little more language support because a question is asked to help the child express a request
Choice prompt (similar to giving choices)	"Would you like the peas or the carrots?"	More language support because the answer can be stated in the question
Say prompt	"Henry, say 'peas.'"	The most support because the adult is telling the child exactly what to say

Adapted from Kaiser, 2011

Prompting your child to use a target word is most appropriate and considerate when he is making a request but not using the target. In Molly's case, taken from the above example, she often resorts to requesting help by making gestures rather than saying the word *help*. Molly's parents may choose to strategically prompt her to say "help."

Dr. Megan Roberts, Dr. Ann Kaiser, and Dr. Courtney Wright, who have extensively studied these strategies, recommend following the subsequent sequence when prompting a child to say a certain word:

1   Begin prompting your child to say a target word by pausing in anticipation and waiting expectantly for the child to request or say something.

2   Next, if the child does not use the target word, ask an open-ended question ("What toy should we play with?").

3   If the child does not respond to the open-ended question, provide him or her with a choice prompt ("Would you like the truck or the blocks?").

4   If the child still does not use a target word, then you can use the prompt, "Say '[target word].'" If your child still does not say the word, then provide the model and say the target word.

Do not overuse prompts during interactions. Prompting more than one time in a minute is *not* recommended. Prompts should not interrupt the flow of conversation, engagement, or play.

As a parent and a practicing speech-language pathologist, I have learned to judiciously prompt. Before doing so, I consider the situation, the toddler's personality, her ability, and mood. For instance, if I sense the toddler is tired or appears to be getting hungry or frustrated, I usually do not progress to level 4. In fact, I rarely use the Say prompt. Prompting a child to say, "say" neither matches my personality nor does it feel like an authentic, two-way communicative exchange. Dr. Susan Lederer, Ph.D, a professor in the Department of Communication Sciences and Disorders at Adelphi University suggests using the phrase, "Tell me". She feels "tell me" is more conversational and naturalistic and less like a direction, "say it because I told you to say it" (Lederer, 2018b). Since learning about Dr. Lederer's suggestion to use "Tell me", I have begun to sporadically say "tell me" when appropriate.

An example of strategically prompting for target words
Molly's mom, Patricia, selected the target word *help*, as Molly infrequently uses this word when she needs assistance. One day, Molly was playing with a windup toy, and she grew frustrated because she could not properly wind it up. She handed the toy to Patricia so she could make it go. Patricia decided to prompt Molly for the word, so when Molly gave her the toy, she paused in anticipation and waited expectantly for a few seconds for Molly to say, "Help." Molly did not say anything, so Patricia then said, "What can

I do for you?" Molly still did not say anything, so Patricia said, "Put away or help?" Molly responded to this choice prompt, "Help." Patricia said, "Yes, I'll help you." If Molly still had not said, "Help," Patricia was prepared to move on to the say prompt (e.g., "Molly, say, 'Help.'").

What is it not?

We should not think of prompting as a way to *force* your child to say a certain word. We want to think of it as a way to encourage the production of preselected target words during highly motivating circumstances. Communication should be fun and functional. Do not overuse these prompting strategies because doing so can lead to frustration and disrupt the natural flow of communication.

An example of prompting for target words gone awry

Let's pretend Patricia woke up on the wrong side of the bed, did not yet have her coffee, and consequently was a little more aggressive with her use of prompting. (This happens to the best of us.) Molly was sitting at the dinner table and desperately trying to poke her fork into her freshly made waffle. She was growing frustrated because she could not get the waffle to stay on the fork. Patricia stepped in; she picked up the fork, paused for a few seconds, and waited expectantly for Molly to say, "Help." Molly did not. Since Patricia did not yet have her coffee and was tired, she decided to jump straight to the say prompt. She said, "Molly, say, 'Help.'" Molly shook her head, yelled, and tried to grab the fork. Patricia then grew frustrated and said again, "Say, 'Help.'" She did this one more time until she finally gave up, poked the waffle with the fork, and gave it to Molly.

Why should we strategically prompt for target words?

Prompts allow children to practice particular language targets in highly motivating situations (Kaiser, 2011). They are especially effective when we are trying to increase the frequency or complexity of words and phrases.

When should we strategically prompt for target words?

Prompting is best used once the child is frequently using intentional communication and has some words or signs in his expressive vocabulary. This is because prompting involves putting some pressure on your child to say a certain word. If a child's imitation skills are still developing, as is their expressive

Please remember that prompting is just one tool in the toolbox. The other seven strategies should also be used to model and elicit first words.

vocabulary, responding to the prompts may be frustrating. Dr. Heather Moore, a speech-language pathologist and clinic supervisor at the University of Oregon, and creator of the Language and Play Everyday (LAPE) Program, believes this type of teaching may be more forceful because it makes the child respond to a prompt rather than initiate on his own. For this reason, she prefers not to use this strategy with children who have less than two hundred words. Children who have less than two hundred words usually have a much harder time imitating or storing and retrieving words from memory (Moore, 2016).

Also, we should strategically prompt for target words only when the child is trying to make a request and is highly motivated to do so.

In my experience, children do best if the prompted words are ones that have been preselected to be target words—the words we are trying to establish in their repertoire or increase in frequency.

How to Create a Language-Rich Environment

AS YOU MAY have guessed from reading thus far, language acquisition is quite complex. Studies have shown that vocabulary development is influenced by many variables, including the child's cognition, executive and memory skills, and environment (Armonia et al., 2015).

The eight techniques for eliciting first words are beneficial in increasing verbal production. However, we should take things a step further by providing our children language-rich environments. A language-rich environment is one where the child has many opportunities to communicate and has much exposure to hearing language.

Children who are provided higher levels of language stimulation early in life, have better language skills than those who are not. Children with better language skills also have a better chance at later achieving academic success. Promoting high-quality language interactions is essential in driving language and communication growth.

> I had given all my patients the same ability to hear, but for those children born into homes where there was less talk, less eliciting of response, less variation in vocabulary, the meaningful sounds needed to make those critical brain connections were not sufficient.
>
> —Dr. Dana Suskind,
> pediatric cochlear implant surgeon
> and founder of the
> Thirty Million Words® Initiative

Here are six ways to create a language-rich environment:

1   Talk more to your child.

2   Read to your child.

3   Sing songs.

4   Go on field trips.

5   Display riveting artwork.

6   Limit screen time.

1. Talk more to your child.

Talking to your child may seem like an obvious way to promote your child's language. In some households, however, children are not spoken to enough. When parents engage in more of what Dr. Todd Risley—a legendary professor, author, and researcher— referred to as "business talk" and less "chitchat" or "conversational talk," they expose their children to far fewer words and their language exchanges are less rich and complex. According to the late Risley, who spent his career researching home-based language learning, business talk consists of "talking to accomplish something" (Risley, n.d.). These include directives, imperatives, and prohibitions like "stop that," "come here," and "hold still." Parents who provide less chitchat or conversational talk have children who hear substantially fewer words. These children are at an academic disadvantage before even entering preschool. But when parents have more back-and-forth conversations, their children are exposed to richer and more varied vocabulary and complex ideas. Researchers from Massachusetts Institute of Technology (MIT) and Harvard recently discovered that these back-and-forth conversational exchanges also change how parts of the brain develop. Using functional magnetic resonance imaging (fMRI), they found that different areas of the brain became more activated when conversational turns increased. Children who engaged in more back-and-forth conversations were observed to have more activity in the Broca's area, a part of the brain involved in language processing and speech production. Furthermore, these children, were also found to score higher on standardized tests evaluating various language components like vocabulary and grammar (Romeo et al., 2018). Therefore, even if it seems one-sided since your little ones may not be speaking as much, have

> Children with strong language skills are more likely to arrive at school ready to learn.
>
> (Snow, Burns, & Griffin, 1998).

conversations with your children. If he makes a sound or even a gesture, react and respond to it as though your child's sound or gesture was part of the conversation.

> It's almost magical how parental conversation appears to influence the biological growth of the brain.
>
> —John Gabrieli, Director of Athinoula A. Martinos Imaging Center at the McGovern Institute

2. Read to your child.

Children learn new words when books are read aloud to them. Vocabulary is learned incidentally because adults are more likely to explain words and concepts during a shared reading activity. Picture books also contain more sophisticated and complex language than is spoken in everyday life. Therefore, reading picture books to your children will expose them to words they may not hear on a daily basis.

Studies also show children benefit from rereading their favorite books. Dr. Jessica Horst from University of Sussex's WORD Lab performed an experiment to see how quickly three-year-olds could identify and remember six new words. Her research revealed that toddlers and preschoolers learned and recalled more new words when the same book was repeatedly read to them. They also learned the words at a faster rate (Levy, 2013). Next time your little one asks to be read the same book, smile and embrace those intimate moments, knowing that familiarity and repetition is good for vocabulary development. For a list of some of my favorite picture books to elicit language from toddlers, please visit www.mytoddlertalks.com and click on my resources.

3. Sing songs.

Singing songs is a great way to develop language. Music helps with language acquisition, because it teaches children about language structure as well as beat and rhythm in a fun way. According to Sally Goddard Blythe, author of *The Genius of Natural Childhood: Secrets of Thriving Children*, ."Neuroimaging has shown music involves more than just centralized hotspots in the brain, occupying large swathes on both sides" (Hill, 2011). Therefore, music uses and develops more parts of the brain, leading to more neurological involvement and improved comprehension. During the first few years of life, it's very important to develop as much of your child's brain as possible.

4. Go on field trips.

Expose your child to new situations and new experiences. With each novel experience, your child has the opportunity to learn new vocabulary. Field trips may be a trip to the lake, beach, zoo, library, park, pet store, coffee shop, or grocery store. These authentic, in-the-moment vocabulary-building experiences assist in developing "wide, flexible, and useful general vocabulary" (Blachowicz, n.d.). This is the type of vocabulary a child needs to communicate effectively and efficiently. Take pictures while on these trips. Show these pictures to your child and talk about them. Go beyond naming names (e.g., "This is a bear."). Explain what someone or something is doing (e.g., "The huge brown bear is eating some berries."). Describe what something or someone looks, feels, or smells like (e.g., "The bear is *huge*. The bear is furry. The bear is strong.").

Two strategies to also use during these trips, and even throughout a typical day, are what speech-language pathologists refer to as self-talk and parallel talk:

- ➤ Self-talk: Talk about what you are doing, eating, touching, or thinking when your child is present and interested. Narrate your actions—for example, "I'm looking at the doggy. Now, I'm petting the doggy. He's such a sweet doggy!"

- ➤ Parallel talk: Talk about what your child is doing, seeing, eating, or touching. Narrate what he is doing—for example, "Johnny's petting the doggy. The doggy's fur is so soft!"

5. Display riveting artwork.

In her book *Raising Passionate Readers: 5 Easy Steps to Success in School and Life*, author Nancy Newman explains how young children spend countless hours at home and how it is "important to pay attention to the interior decoration of your child's brain, heart, and soul by talking with him" (2014, 52). She suggests adding some "snap and sizzle" to verbal exchanges by "hanging interesting pictures, postcards, maps, or photographs on walls and on the refrigerator and chatting about them." This is such an easy way to stimulate your child's occipital lobe and visual processing system. Hang these conversational art pieces in places where your toddler will notice, perhaps by the changing table, on a coffee table, bathroom mirror, nightstand, or refrigerator. Take it a step further by having your toddler help you sort through all the mail, too. We receive cards, brochures, magazines, and other colorful junk mail that my little one loves to rip open and "read." If you are looking for some ideas and appreciate realistic art with touches of whimsy and wonder, I highly recommend author and illustrator Nancy Tillman's artwork.

6. Limit screen time.

In today's world, screens can surround us twenty-four hours a day, seven days a week. Sometimes it seems like we cannot escape screens. Screen time refers to more than just watching television. It includes phones, iPads, smartly marketed "educational" learning tablets for children, the DVD player in the car, movie theaters, and even some fancy watches. More screen time equals less face-to-face, direct interaction. Studies show that children learn language from direct human interaction, *not* screens. You interact and talk to your child less when he is watching a screen. Furthermore, too much screen time can actually harm your child. It can negatively impact attention and focus, behavior, sleep quality, social skills, and even language growth. According to a case control study by Dr. Weerasak Chonchaiya and Dr. Chandhita Pruksananonda, children who started watching television before twelve months old, and watched more than two hours of television per day, were six times more likely to have language delays. (Chonchaiya & Pruksananonda, 2008). Another more recent study of 119 Hispanic infants and toddlers further supported that too much screen time has a "deleterious" impact on language growth. It was found that children who watched more than two hours of television a day had a greater chance of having low communication scores (Duch et al., 2013).

> The AAP recommends parents prioritize creative, unplugged playtime for infants and toddlers. Some media can have educational value for children starting at around eighteen months of age, but it's critically important that this be high-quality programming, such as the content offered by Sesame Workshop and PBS. Parents of young children should watch media with their child to help children understand what they are seeing.
>
> —American Academy of Pediatrics, 2016

New research by psychologists from Temple University and the University of Delaware also have found that when cell phone calls interrupt parents from interacting with their children, their children are less likely to learn a new target word than if they were not interrupted with a phone call. Their study builds on previous research supporting that toddlers "are sensitive to disruptions within the dynamic flow of a word-learning task" (Reed, Hirsh-Pasek & Golinkoff, 2017, p. 1429). Thus, it is equally important for parents to limit their use of screens, phones, and tablets when interacting with children, especially when the focus is on word learning. Toddlers learn language when they are fully engaged with a responsive and attentive communication partner.

The American Academy of Pediatrics updated in October 2016 their recommendations for children's media use. Please see table 5 on the following page for some of their recommendations:

TABLE 5: **The American Academy of Pediatrics Screen-Time Recommendations for Children and Families**

AGE	RECOMMENDATIONS
Eighteen months and younger	Provide no screen time other than video chatting.
Eighteen to twenty-four months	Choose high-quality programming and watch with children "to help them understand what they're seeing."
Two to five years old	Limit screen use to one hour per day of high-quality programs, and watch programs with children to help them understand what they are seeing and make connections to their own lives.
Six years and older	Limit the amount and type of screen time, and ensure it does not negatively impact sleep, attention, and behavior and does not decrease or replace physical activity.
General recommendations: Create screen-free times, such as when eating meals, driving in the car, or riding in the stroller, and establish screen-free locations, such as bedrooms and the dining room.	

As a parent, I know it can be difficult to fully eliminate screen time, but if your child has a language delay, I recommend trying a 30-day screen diet. Try doing this when you begin your 30-day journaling endeavor. After all, screen time feeds your child's brain empty calories. Instead, feed your child's brain nutrient-dense calories in the form of conversation, interaction, and play. If you need assistance in creating a family screen-time plan, the American Academy of Pediatrics created an online Family Media Use Plan Tool that is available for free at www.healthychildren.org/MediaUsePlan. If you would like some suggestions on how to replace screen time, please visit www.mytoddlertalks.com/howtoreplacescreentime.

Encouraging a Reluctant Toddler

I F YOU HAVE seen the award winning film, Forrest Gump, you probably recall when he says, "Life is like a box of chocolates, you never know what you're going to get." Toddlers are the same way. They are very unpredictable and full of surprises. There will be many times when your toddler does not want to say a target word. When it happens, I encourage you to be flexible and opportunistic. Work with what your child gives you. If your toddler is not responding to your attempts to elicit your carefully chosen target word, you may have to tweak your plan a bit.

Researchers from the University of Washington Speech and Hearing Clinic who were studying lexical and phonological aspects of early word production sometimes had to abandon preselected target words when the children did not show any "interest in an object that was intended to elicit a specific target word but spontaneously produced a possible target word that had not originally been selected for that child" (Sosa & Stoel-Gammon, 2012, p. 600). The investigators then had to select different target words based on what the child spontaneously said instead. If you're trying to get your child to say "toast," his favorite breakfast food, but he is refusing to say it, instead notice what he is trying to say. If he is pointing to, gesturing, or trying to say, "Hot," or "Butter," instead of "Toast," then these are your child's new targets.

Furthermore, research suggests that children who have learned individual words through targeted, repeated training then go on to learn *many* words at once (Gershkoff-Stowe & Hahn, 2007). This momentum is believed to occur because the repeated practice strengthens children's underlying vocabulary system, priming them to learn more words. It is easier to acquire new words when one already has some in her vocabulary. This is because linking, connecting, or associating the new word

to a word already in one's lexicon is a faster process. A toddler who likes pizza and says, "Pizza" (or an approximation of this word) may have an easier time understanding and conveying it is something eaten that is hot, yummy, and made of cheese.

Remember: your end goal is to promote overall word learning and communication.

PART FOUR

Make It Happen
The 30-Day Workbook

Instructions for the 30-Day Workbook

LET'S MAKE IT happen and put everything we learned into practice by using the 30-Day Workbook. The 30-Day Workbook is divided into four-week sections. Each week includes a weekly plan of attack example to clearly show you how to proceed over the next seven days. Within each week there are seven days where you can record what you did to jump-start your toddler's language. The questions and prompts for the daily entries are consistent to keep you focused on developing your skills without distraction. The motivational quotes and fun facts that are included on the daily entries are unique to keep your interest.

Begin each week by looking at your "Master List of Initial Words to Target." Depending on your toddler's current inventory of spoken words, choose one to three words to target over the next week. Take about ten to fifteen minutes to thoughtfully answer the questions in the checklist format (e.g., Are these words developmentally appropriate and motivating to my toddler and/or do they mesh well with our family dynamic? What will these words help my toddler to do?, What technique(s) will I practice this week to target this word/these words? etc.)

Many of my clients like to spend ten to fifteen minutes the night before the week begins, thinking about how and when they will use the techniques and recommendations in this book. For instance, they will take time on a Sunday night to come up with a plan on what to target starting on Monday.

At the end of each day, if you have time, spend another ten to fifteen minutes responding to questions in the workbook. Many spouses or partners like doing this together before retiring for the evening. If you are pressed for time, quickly jot down a few notes about your efforts to stimulate your toddler's language on the condensed daily entry form.

At the end of the week, or on the seventh day of the week, there is a "Weekly Update" form. This is where you can thoughtfully think about what you did during the whole week to encourage your toddler's language.

This same process repeats for the next three weeks.

At the end of 30 days, recap your effort and review your 30-Day language-stimulation adventure with your special toddler.

WHO:

Marie, an eighteen-month-old girl

TARGET WORD(S):

"Up" to request when she wants to be picked up and to comment when something goes up or is located up (in the sky, in a tree, etc.)

TECHNIQUE TO PRACTICE:

Pause in anticipation before picking her up

DAILY ROUTINES FOCUSED ON:

Getting into her car seat, getting into her high chair, and going up the stairs

SONG TO SING:

"Hickory Dickory Dock," emphasizing the verses "...went *up* the clock" and using hand gestures to indicate up while singing the song

BOOK TO READ:

Ten Apples Up on Top! by Dr. Seuss, Theo LeSieg, and Roy McKie

OTHER:

When blowing bubbles (e.g., "They go up, up, up.") or throwing a ball ("It goes up, up, up.")

GOALS FOR WEEK 1

➤ My target word(s) for the week will be

_____

➤ Are these words developmentally appropriate and motivating to my toddler, and/or do they mesh well with our family dynamic?

☐ Yes ☐ No

➤ What will these words help my toddler to do? Check the communicative function(s).

☐ Request ☐ Comment

☐ Reject or protest ☐ Ask questions

☐ Label ☐ Socially interact and connect

➤ What technique(s) will I practice this week to target this word/these words? Check the technique(s).

☐ Identify and appreciate the child's lead ☐ Give choices

☐ Be responsive ☐ Imitate, imitate, imitate

☐ Pause in anticipation ☐ Create predictable play routines

☐ Set it up ☐ Strategically prompt for target words

➤ This week, I will embed the language technique(s) and focus on using the target(s) during the following daily routine(s):

☐ Going potty ☐ Getting ready for a nap

☐ Brushing teeth ☐ Sorting and washing laundry and folding clothes

☐ Washing hands

☐ Getting dressed ☐ Playing

☐ Preparing and eating a meal or snack ☐ Reading a book

☐ Taking a bath

☐ Getting ready to leave the house ☐ Getting ready for bed

☐ Getting into and riding in the car ☐ Other daily routine:

_____

☐ Shopping at a store _____

☐ Going to _____ (name of destination) _____

☐ Changing diapers

WEEK 1: *"It was great when…" "I need to work on…" "Next time, I will…"*

MONDAY	**TUESDAY**
WEDNESDAY	**THURSDAY**
FRIDAY	**SATURDAY**
SUNDAY	**NOTES**

WEEK 1: Day 1

Date_____

> Children don't need more things. The best toys a child can have is a parent who gets down on the floor and plays with them.
>
> —Dr. Bruce Perry, MD, PhD

What three things did I do today to encourage my toddler's first words?

Examples: Did I use a particular strategy or technique? Did we play a certain game or perform a special play routine? Did I infuse language and purposefully use specific target words in my daily routines?

1 _____

2 _____

3 _____

What did my toddler say or do in response to these three things?

Examples: My toddler looked at me, smiled, and tried to say, "Open" when I waited expectantly for him. My toddler gestured "all done" when she was finished playing with the playhouse. My toddler gave me his toy car when I said, "Oh, I like your car!"

1 _____

2 _____

3 _____

Could I have done or said anything differently?

Examples: Maybe I should have waited until I had my toddler's full attention before I expected him to follow my direction. Maybe I was talking too much and didn't give my child enough time to initiate communication. Perhaps my toddler didn't have enough opportunities to hear the target word.

_____

_____

_____

What will I do tomorrow to stimulate or further develop my toddler's first words?

Examples: Try a different strategy. Try the same strategy but do it consistently through my toddler's daily routines. Try a different play routine.

_____

_____

_____

What questions or comments do I have for my toddler's speech-language pathologist, teacher, or other professional?

_____

_____

Day 2

Date_____

What three things did I do today to encourage my toddler's first words?

Examples: Did I use a particular strategy or technique? Did we play a certain game or perform a special play routine? Did I infuse language and purposefully use specific target words in my daily routines?

1 _____

_____

2 _____

_____

3 _____

_____

> Accept quiet times or quiet moments. There will be instances when your child is just quiet. Often, children can be quiet when they are learning and processing new information or when they have been introduced to a new toy or novel play routine.

What did my toddler say or do in response to these three things?

Examples: My toddler looked at me, smiled, and tried to say, "Open" when I waited expectantly for him. My toddler gestured "all done" when she was finished playing with the playhouse. My toddler gave me his toy car when I said, "Oh, I like your car!"

1 _____

_____

2 _____

_____

3 _____

_____

Could I have done or said anything differently?

Examples: Maybe I should have waited until I had my toddler's full attention before I expected him to follow my direction. Maybe I was talking too much and didn't give my child enough time to initiate communication. Perhaps my toddler didn't have enough opportunities to hear the target word.

_____

_____

_____

What will I do tomorrow to stimulate or further develop my toddler's first words?

Examples: Try a different strategy. Try the same strategy but do it consistently through my toddler's daily routines. Try a different play routine.

_____

_____

_____

What questions or comments do I have for my toddler's speech-language pathologist, teacher, or other professional?

_____

_____

_____

Day 3

Date_____

Involve your whole child in an activity. Research supports that movement increases children's overall development. According to Kendra Moyses, an educator with Michigan State University Extension, "When language is combined with movement, learning increases 90 percent."

(Moyses, 2012)

What three things did I do today to encourage my toddler's first words?

Examples: Did I use a particular strategy or technique? Did we play a certain game or perform a special play routine? Did I infuse language and purposefully use specific target words in my daily routines?

1 _____

_____

2 _____

_____

3 _____

_____

What did my toddler say or do in response to these three things?

Examples: My toddler looked at me, smiled, and tried to say, "Open" when I waited expectantly for him. My toddler gestured "all done" when she was finished playing with the playhouse. My toddler gave me his toy car when I said, "Oh, I like your car!"

1 _____

_____

2 _____

_____

3 _____

_____

Could I have done or said anything differently?

Examples: Maybe I should have waited until I had my toddler's full attention before I expected him to follow my direction. Maybe I was talking too much and didn't give my child enough time to initiate communication. Perhaps my toddler didn't have enough opportunities to hear the target word.

_____

_____

_____

What will I do tomorrow to stimulate or further develop my toddler's first words? Examples: Try a different strategy. Try the same strategy but do it consistently through my toddler's daily routines. Try a different play routine.

_____

_____

_____

What questions or comments do I have for my toddler's speech-language pathologist, teacher, or other professional?

_____

_____

_____

Day 4

Date_____

What three things did I do today to encourage my toddler's first words?

Examples: Did I use a particular strategy or technique? Did we play a certain game or perform a special play routine? Did I infuse language and purposefully use specific target words in my daily routines?

1 _____

_____

2 _____

_____

3 _____

_____

> Tell me and I forget. Teach me and I remember. Involve me and I learn.
>
> —Benjamin Franklin

What did my toddler say or do in response to these three things?

Examples: My toddler looked at me, smiled, and tried to say, "Open" when I waited expectantly for him. My toddler gestured "all done" when she was finished playing with the playhouse. My toddler gave me his toy car when I said, "Oh, I like your car!"

1 _____

_____

2 _____

_____

3 _____

_____

Could I have done or said anything differently?

Examples: Maybe I should have waited until I had my toddler's full attention before I expected him to follow my direction. Maybe I was talking too much and didn't give my child enough time to initiate communication. Perhaps my toddler didn't have enough opportunities to hear the target word.

_____

_____

_____

What will I do tomorrow to stimulate or further develop my toddler's first words?

Examples: Try a different strategy. Try the same strategy but do it consistently through my toddler's daily routines. Try a different play routine.

_____

_____

_____

What questions or comments do I have for my toddler's speech-language pathologist, teacher, or other professional?

_____

_____

_____

Day 5

Date_____

If your toddler is not yet talking, be especially observant and notice what your toddler is looking at, pointing to, or interested in. If he or she is interested in something, he or she will want to know more about it. Talk about it.

What three things did I do today to encourage my toddler's first words?

Examples: Did I use a particular strategy or technique? Did we play a certain game or perform a special play routine? Did I infuse language and purposefully use specific target words in my daily routines?

1 _____

_____

2 _____

_____

3 _____

_____

What did my toddler say or do in response to these three things?

Examples: My toddler looked at me, smiled, and tried to say, "Open" when I waited expectantly for him. My toddler gestured "all done" when she was finished playing with the playhouse. My toddler gave me his toy car when I said, "Oh, I like your car!"

1 _____

_____

2 _____

_____

3 _____

_____

Could I have done or said anything differently?

Examples: Maybe I should have waited until I had my toddler's full attention before I expected him to follow my direction. Maybe I was talking too much and didn't give my child enough time to initiate communication. Perhaps my toddler didn't have enough opportunities to hear the target word.

_____

_____

_____

What will I do tomorrow to stimulate or further develop my toddler's first words?

Examples: Try a different strategy. Try the same strategy but do it consistently through my toddler's daily routines. Try a different play routine.

_____

_____

_____

What questions or comments do I have for my toddler's speech-language pathologist, teacher, or other professional?

_____

_____

_____

Day 6

Date_____

What three things did I do today to encourage my toddler's first words?

Examples: Did I use a particular strategy or technique? Did we play a certain game or perform a special play routine? Did I infuse language and purposefully use specific target words in my daily routines?

1 _____

_____

2 _____

_____

3 _____

_____

> **Did you know?** Fetuses can begin to learn language in the womb. Research suggests that unborn babies hear and process sounds heard in the womb.
>
> (Skwarecki, 2013)

What did my toddler say or do in response to these three things?

Examples: My toddler looked at me, smiled, and tried to say, "Open" when I waited expectantly for him. My toddler gestured "all done" when she was finished playing with the playhouse. My toddler gave me his toy car when I said, "Oh, I like your car!"

1 _____

_____

2 _____

_____

3 _____

_____

Could I have done or said anything differently?

Examples: Maybe I should have waited until I had my toddler's full attention before I expected him to follow my direction. Maybe I was talking too much and didn't give my child enough time to initiate communication. Perhaps my toddler didn't have enough opportunities to hear the target word.

_____

_____

_____

What will I do tomorrow to stimulate or further develop my toddler's first words?

Examples: Try a different strategy. Try the same strategy but do it consistently through my toddler's daily routines. Try a different play routine.

_____

_____

_____

What questions or comments do I have for my toddler's speech-language pathologist, teacher, or other professional?

_____

_____

_____

Day 7

Date_____

> It's a marathon, not a sprint.

What three things did I do today to encourage my toddler's first words?

Examples: Did I use a particular strategy or technique? Did we play a certain game or perform a special play routine? Did I infuse language and purposefully use specific target words in my daily routines?

1 _____

_____

2 _____

_____

3 _____

_____

What did my toddler say or do in response to these three things?

Examples: My toddler looked at me, smiled, and tried to say, "Open" when I waited expectantly for him. My toddler gestured "all done" when she was finished playing with the playhouse. My toddler gave me his toy car when I said, "Oh, I like your car!"

1 _____

_____

2 _____

_____

3 _____

_____

Could I have done or said anything differently?

Examples: Maybe I should have waited until I had my toddler's full attention before I expected him to follow my direction. Maybe I was talking too much and didn't give my child enough time to initiate communication. Perhaps my toddler didn't have enough opportunities to hear the target word.

_____

_____

_____

What will I do tomorrow to stimulate or further develop my toddler's first words?

Examples: Try a different strategy. Try the same strategy but do it consistently through my toddler's daily routines. Try a different play routine.

_____

_____

_____

What questions or comments do I have for my toddler's speech-language pathologist, teacher, or other professional?

_____

_____

_____

Weekly Update

How Am I Doing?
How have I improved my ability to encourage communication, first words, and interaction with my toddler?

_____

_____

_____

_____

How Is My Toddler Doing?
How is my toddler becoming a more effective communicator? What new first words is he or she more regularly saying? Are any previously spoken words being said more frequently or with better clarity?

_____

_____

_____

_____

My Goals for Next Week:

I will work on using _____ (name of technique) during

_____ (name daily routine or

specific play activity) and will focus on having my toddler say or

do _____ _____ (selected target word

or other goal suggested by my speech-language pathologist).

Superstar Highlight from This Week!

It made me smile when

_____

_____

_____

_____

_____

_____

Every night, after dinner and before bath, my son and I play together for about fifteen to thirty minutes. Not being able to see him during the day since I work, this became our special time. He really enjoyed being wrapped up like a burrito with the blankets. So we tended to play this burrito game, and I was able to consistently target the words roll, up, and down. After doing this every day for about two weeks, Samuel is now saying these words all by himself!

—Father of Samuel, aged thirty-four months

GOALS FOR WEEK 2

➤ My target word(s) for the week will be

_____

➤ Are these words developmentally appropriate and motivating to my toddler, and/or do they mesh well with our family dynamic?

☐ Yes   ☐ No

➤ What will these words help my toddler to do? Check the communicative function(s).

☐ Request   ☐ Comment

☐ Reject or protest   ☐ Ask questions

☐ Label   ☐ Socially interact and connect

➤ What technique(s) will I practice this week to target this word/these words? Check the technique(s).

☐ Identify and appreciate the child's lead   ☐ Give choices

☐ Be responsive   ☐ Imitate, imitate, imitate

☐ Pause in anticipation   ☐ Create predictable play routines

☐ Set it up   ☐ Strategically prompt for target words

➤ This week, I will embed the language technique(s) and focus on using the target(s) during the following daily routine(s):

☐ Going potty

☐ Brushing teeth

☐ Washing hands

☐ Getting dressed

☐ Preparing and eating a meal or snack

☐ Getting ready to leave the house

☐ Getting into and riding in the car

☐ Shopping at a store

☐ Going to _____ (name of destination)

☐ Changing diapers

☐ Getting ready for a nap

☐ Sorting and washing laundry and folding clothes

☐ Playing

☐ Reading a book

☐ Taking a bath

☐ Getting ready for bed

☐ Other daily routine:

_____

_____

_____

WEEK 2: *"I see improvement with..." "I'll follow his lead by..."*
"Every time we eat, I'll..."

MONDAY	TUESDAY
WEDNESDAY	THURSDAY
FRIDAY	SATURDAY
SUNDAY	NOTES

Week 2: Day 8

Date_____

> Learning interactions in these early years should be fun and playful. keep things engaging and exciting by not putting too much pressure on your child to perform a certain way.

What three things did I do today to encourage my toddler's first words?
Examples: Did I use a particular strategy or technique? Did we play a certain game or perform a special play routine? Did I infuse language and purposefully use specific target words in my daily routines?

1 _____

_____

2 _____

_____

3 _____

_____

What did my toddler say or do in response to these three things?
Examples: My toddler looked at me, smiled, and tried to say, "Open" when I waited expectantly for him. My toddler gestured "all done" when she was finished playing with the playhouse. My toddler gave me his toy car when I said, "Oh, I like your car!"

1 _____

_____

2 _____

_____

3 _____

_____

Could I have done or said anything differently?
Examples: Maybe I should have waited until I had my toddler's full attention before I expected him to follow my direction. Maybe I was talking too much and didn't give my child enough time to initiate communication. Perhaps my toddler didn't have enough opportunities to hear the target word.

_____

_____

_____

What will I do tomorrow to stimulate or further develop my toddler's first words?
Examples: Try a different strategy. Try the same strategy but do it consistently through my toddler's daily routines. Try a different play routine.

_____

_____

_____

What questions or comments do I have for my toddler's speech-language pathologist, teacher, or other professional?

_____

_____

_____

Day 9

Date_____

What three things did I do today to encourage my toddler's first words?
Examples: Did I use a particular strategy or technique? Did we play a certain game or perform a special play routine? Did I infuse language and purposefully use specific target words in my daily routines?

1 _____

_____

2 _____

_____

3 _____

_____

Did you know? Toddlers aren't expected to say words perfectly. Norms vary, but typically by four years of age, most children are 100 percent intelligible to strangers. At this age, they may still mispronounce some words but are able to be understood.

What did my toddler say or do in response to these three things?
Examples: My toddler looked at me, smiled, and tried to say, "Open" when I waited expectantly for him. My toddler gestured "all done" when she was finished playing with the playhouse. My toddler gave me his toy car when I said, "Oh, I like your car!"

1 _____

_____

2 _____

_____

3 _____

_____

Could I have done or said anything differently?
Examples: Maybe I should have waited until I had my toddler's full attention before I expected him to follow my direction. Maybe I was talking too much and didn't give my child enough time to initiate communication. Perhaps my toddler didn't have enough opportunities to hear the target word.

_____

_____

_____

What will I do tomorrow to stimulate or further develop my toddler's first words?
Examples: Try a different strategy. Try the same strategy but do it consistently through my toddler's daily routines. Try a different play routine.

_____

_____

_____

What questions or comments do I have for my toddler's speech-language pathologist, teacher, or other professional?

_____

_____

_____

Day 10

Date_____

> Play gives children a chance to practice what they are learning.
>
> —Fred Rogers

What three things did I do today to encourage my toddler's first words?

Examples: Did I use a particular strategy or technique? Did we play a certain game or perform a special play routine? Did I infuse language and purposefully use specific target words in my daily routines?

1 _____

_____

2 _____

_____

3 _____

_____

What did my toddler say or do in response to these three things?

Examples: My toddler looked at me, smiled, and tried to say, "Open" when I waited expectantly for him. My toddler gestured "all done" when she was finished playing with the playhouse. My toddler gave me his toy car when I said, "Oh, I like your car!"

1 _____

_____

2 _____

_____

3 _____

_____

Could I have done or said anything differently?

Examples: Maybe I should have waited until I had my toddler's full attention before I expected him to follow my direction. Maybe I was talking too much and didn't give my child enough time to initiate communication. Perhaps my toddler didn't have enough opportunities to hear the target word.

_____

_____

_____

What will I do tomorrow to stimulate or further develop my toddler's first words?

Examples: Try a different strategy. Try the same strategy but do it consistently through my toddler's daily routines. Try a different play routine.

_____

_____

_____

What questions or comments do I have for my toddler's speech-language pathologist, teacher, or other professional?

_____

_____

_____

Day 11

What three things did I do today to encourage my toddler's first words?

Examples: Did I use a particular strategy or technique? Did we play a certain game or perform a special play routine? Did I infuse language and purposefully use specific target words in my daily routines?

1 _____

_____

2 _____

_____

3 _____

_____

> When reading a book to your toddler, be animated and use inflection to stress certain words. Doing this increases your child's attention and further facilitates encoding and recall.

What did my toddler say or do in response to these three things?

Examples: My toddler looked at me, smiled, and tried to say, "Open" when I waited expectantly for him. My toddler gestured "all done" when she was finished playing with the playhouse. My toddler gave me his toy car when I said, "Oh, I like your car!"

1 _____

_____

2 _____

_____

3 _____

_____

Could I have done or said anything differently?

Examples: Maybe I should have waited until I had my toddler's full attention before I expected him to follow my direction. Maybe I was talking too much and didn't give my child enough time to initiate communication. Perhaps my toddler didn't have enough opportunities to hear the target word.

_____

_____

_____

What will I do tomorrow to stimulate or further develop my toddler's first words?

Examples: Try a different strategy. Try the same strategy but do it consistently through my toddler's daily routines. Try a different play routine.

_____

_____

_____

What questions or comments do I have for my toddler's speech-language pathologist, teacher, or other professional?

_____

_____

_____

Day 12

Date_____

Did you know? A noisy environment can hamper a child's ability to acquire new vocabulary and learn new words. Noise makes it difficult to adequately perceive speech (Did mom say "cat" or "bat"?). It can also negatively affect the encoding and storage of new words. This is because the brain works so hard filtering out the noise that it spends less time focusing on and processing the new content.

(McMillan & Saffran, 2016)

What three things did I do today to encourage my toddler's first words?

Examples: Did I use a particular strategy or technique? Did we play a certain game or perform a special play routine? Did I infuse language and purposefully use specific target words in my daily routines?

1 _____

_____

2 _____

_____

3 _____

_____

What did my toddler say or do in response to these three things?

Examples: My toddler looked at me, smiled, and tried to say, "Open" when I waited expectantly for him. My toddler gestured "all done" when she was finished playing with the playhouse. My toddler gave me his toy car when I said, "Oh, I like your car!"

1 _____

_____

2 _____

_____

3 _____

_____

Could I have done or said anything differently?

Examples: Maybe I should have waited until I had my toddler's full attention before I expected him to follow my direction. Maybe I was talking too much and didn't give my child enough time to initiate communication. Perhaps my toddler didn't have enough opportunities to hear the target word.

_____

_____

_____

What will I do tomorrow to stimulate or further develop my toddler's first words?

Examples: Try a different strategy. Try the same strategy but do it consistently through my toddler's daily routines. Try a different play routine.

_____

_____

What questions or comments do I have for my toddler's speech-language pathologist, teacher, or other professional?

_____

_____

Day 13

Date_____

What three things did I do today to encourage my toddler's first words?

Examples: Did I use a particular strategy or technique? Did we play a certain game or perform a special play routine? Did I infuse language and purposefully use specific target words in my daily routines?

1 _____

_____

2 _____

_____

3 _____

_____

> The way we talk to our children becomes their inner voice.
>
> —Peggy O'Mara,
> author of *Natural Family Living*

What did my toddler say or do in response to these three things?

Examples: My toddler looked at me, smiled, and tried to say, "Open" when I waited expectantly for him. My toddler gestured "all done" when she was finished playing with the playhouse. My toddler gave me his toy car when I said, "Oh, I like your car!"

1 _____

_____

2 _____

_____

3 _____

_____

Could I have done or said anything differently?

Examples: Maybe I should have waited until I had my toddler's full attention before I expected him to follow my direction. Maybe I was talking too much and didn't give my child enough time to initiate communication. Perhaps my toddler didn't have enough opportunities to hear the target word.

_____

_____

_____

What will I do tomorrow to stimulate or further develop my toddler's first words?

Examples: Try a different strategy. Try the same strategy but do it consistently through my toddler's daily routines. Try a different play routine.

_____

_____

_____

What questions or comments do I have for my toddler's speech-language pathologist, teacher, or other professional?

_____

_____

_____

Day 14

Date_____

Three questions to ask yourself:

1) Does this interaction feel natural and authentic?

2) If I were in my toddler's place, would I want to talk to me?

3) Am I overusing the techniques so that there are no breaks for silence and reflection?

What three things did I do today to encourage my toddler's first words?
Examples: Did I use a particular strategy or technique? Did we play a certain game or perform a special play routine? Did I infuse language and purposefully use specific target words in my daily routines?

1 _____

_____

2 _____

_____

3 _____

_____

What did my toddler say or do in response to these three things?
Examples: My toddler looked at me, smiled, and tried to say, "Open" when I waited expectantly for him. My toddler gestured "all done" when she was finished playing with the playhouse. My toddler gave me his toy car when I said, "Oh, I like your car!"

1 _____

_____

2 _____

_____

3 _____

_____

Could I have done or said anything differently?
Examples: Maybe I should have waited until I had my toddler's full attention before I expected him to follow my direction. Maybe I was talking too much and didn't give my child enough time to initiate communication. Perhaps my toddler didn't have enough opportunities to hear the target word.

_____

_____

_____

What will I do tomorrow to stimulate or further develop my toddler's first words?
Examples: Try a different strategy. Try the same strategy but do it consistently through my toddler's daily routines. Try a different play routine.

_____

_____

_____

What questions or comments do I have for my toddler's speech-language pathologist, teacher, or other professional?

_____

_____

_____

Weekly Update

How Am I Doing?
How have I improved my ability to encourage communication, first words, and interaction with my toddler?

_____

_____

_____

_____

How Is My Toddler Doing?
How is my toddler becoming a more effective communicator? What new first words is he or she more regularly saying? Are any previously spoken words being said more frequently or with better clarity?

_____

_____

_____

_____

My Goals for Next Week:

I will work on using _____ (name of technique) during

_____ (name daily routine or

specific play activity) and will focus on having my toddler say or

do _____ _____ (selected target word

or other goal suggested by my speech-language pathologist).

Superstar Highlight from This Week!

It made me smile when

_____

_____

_____

_____

_____

_____

As a single mother, I have to work, so my little girl is in day care about forty hours a week. Every day, I try my best to playfully interact and play with Madison to build her language, but it was really important for me to make sure that her day care providers knew how to stimulate her language too. Every week, I made copies of the weekly goals sheet and gave a copy to her teacher, Ms. Susie. She was more than happy to help, and it was great to know that Madison was getting support at her day care too.

—Mother of Madison,
aged twenty-nine months

Weekly Plan of Attack Example

WHO:

Luna, a twenty-six-month-old girl

TARGET WORD(S):

"Cheese" (one of Luna's favorite foods to eat)

TECHNIQUE TO PRACTICE:

Give choices

DAILY ROUTINES FOCUSED ON:

Mealtimes and snack

SONG TO SING:

"On Top of Spaghetti" ("...all covered in *cheese...*") and "The Farmer in the Dell" ("...the mouse takes the *cheese...*")

BOOK TO READ:

More Cheese, Please! by Sue Kueffner

GOALS FOR WEEK 3

➤ My target word(s) for the week will be

_____

➤ Are these words developmentally appropriate and motivating to my toddler, and/or do they mesh well with our family dynamic?

    ☐ Yes   ☐ No

➤ What will these words help my toddler to do? Check the communicative function(s).

☐ Request   ☐ Comment

☐ Reject or protest   ☐ Ask questions

☐ Label   ☐ Socially interact and connect

➤ What technique(s) will I practice this week to target this word/these words? Check the technique(s).

☐ Identify and appreciate the child's lead   ☐ Give choices

☐ Be responsive   ☐ Imitate, imitate, imitate

☐ Pause in anticipation   ☐ Create predictable play routines

☐ Set it up   ☐ Strategically prompt for target words

➤ This week, I will embed the language technique(s) and focus on using the target(s) during the following daily routine(s):

☐ Going potty   ☐ Getting ready for a nap

☐ Brushing teeth   ☐ Sorting and washing laundry and folding clothes

☐ Washing hands

☐ Getting dressed   ☐ Playing

☐ Preparing and eating a meal or snack   ☐ Reading a book

☐ Getting ready to leave the house   ☐ Taking a bath

     ☐ Getting ready for bed

☐ Getting into and riding in the car   ☐ Other daily routine:

☐ Shopping at a store   _____

☐ Going to _____ (name of destination)   _____

☐ Changing diapers

WEEK 3: *"I'll keep trying to..." "What strategy did I use?" "I kept it fun by..."*

MONDAY	TUESDAY
WEDNESDAY	THURSDAY
FRIDAY	SATURDAY
SUNDAY	NOTES

Week 3: Day 15

Date_____

> Work on growing your child's vocabulary, but don't focus on adding only nouns (aka persons, places, or things). Stress tangible action words, observable describing words, and salient location words.

What three things did I do today to encourage my toddler's first words?

Examples: Did I use a particular strategy or technique? Did we play a certain game or perform a special play routine? Did I infuse language and purposefully use specific target words in my daily routines?

1 _____

_____

2 _____

_____

3 _____

What did my toddler say or do in response to these three things?

Examples: My toddler looked at me, smiled, and tried to say "open," when I waited expectantly for him. My toddler gestured "all done" when she was finished playing with the playhouse. My toddler gave me his toy car when I said, "Oh, I like your car!"

1 _____

_____

2 _____

_____

3 _____

_____

Could I have done or said anything differently?

Examples: Maybe I should have waited until I had my toddler's full attention before I expected him to follow my direction. Maybe I was talking too much and didn't give my child enough time to initiate communication. Perhaps my toddler didn't have enough opportunities to hear the target word.

_____

_____

_____

What will I do tomorrow to stimulate or further develop my toddler's first words?

Examples: Try a different strategy. Try the same strategy but do it consistently through my toddler's daily routines. Try a different play routine.

_____

_____

_____

What questions or comments do I have for my toddler's speech-language pathologist, teacher, or other professional?

_____

_____

_____

Day 16

Date_____

What three things did I do today to encourage my toddler's first words?

Examples: Did I use a particular strategy or technique? Did we play a certain game or perform a special play routine? Did I infuse language and purposefully use specific target words in my daily routines?

1 _____

_____

2 _____

_____

3 _____

_____

What did my toddler say or do in response to these three things?

Examples: My toddler looked at me, smiled, and tried to say, "Open" when I waited expectantly for him. My toddler gestured "all done" when she was finished playing with the playhouse. My toddler gave me his toy car when I said, "Oh, I like your car!"

1 _____

_____

2 _____

_____

3 _____

_____

> Did you know? Recent research published in the *Journal of the American Medical Association Pediatrics* revealed that parents were most responsive to their children when engaging in traditional play, not play with electronic toys, and when reading books together. The more responsive you are during play, the more language opportunities you create for your child.
>
> (Sosa, 2015)

Could I have done or said anything differently?

Examples: Maybe I should have waited until I had my toddler's full attention before I expected him to follow my direction. Maybe I was talking too much and didn't give my child enough time to initiate communication. Perhaps my toddler didn't have enough opportunities to hear the target word.

_____

_____

_____

What will I do tomorrow to stimulate or further develop my toddler's first words?

Examples: Try a different strategy. Try the same strategy but do it consistently through my toddler's daily routines. Try a different play routine.

_____

_____

What questions or comments do I have for my toddler's speech-language pathologist, teacher, or other professional?

_____

_____

Day 17

Date_____

> Each day of our lives we make deposits in the memory banks of our children.
>
> —Charles R. Swindoll,
> Pastor, author, and educator

What three things did I do today to encourage my toddler's first words?
Examples: Did I use a particular strategy or technique? Did we play a certain game or perform a special play routine? Did I infuse language and purposefully use specific target words in my daily routines?

1 _____

_____

2 _____

3 _____

_____

What did my toddler say or do in response to these three things?
Examples: My toddler looked at me, smiled, and tried to say, "Open" when I waited expectantly for him. My toddler gestured "all done" when she was finished playing with the playhouse. My toddler gave me his toy car when I said, "Oh, I like your car!"

1 _____

_____

2 _____

_____

3 _____

_____

Could I have done or said anything differently?
Examples: Maybe I should have waited until I had my toddler's full attention before I expected him to follow my direction. Maybe I was talking too much and didn't give my child enough time to initiate communication. Perhaps my toddler did not have enough opportunities to hear the target word.

_____

_____

_____

What will I do tomorrow to stimulate or further develop my toddler's first words?
Examples: Try a different strategy. Try the same strategy but do it consistently through my toddler's daily routines. Try a different play routine.

_____

_____

_____

What questions or comments do I have for my toddler's speech-language pathologist, teacher, or other professional?

_____

_____

_____

Day 18

Date_____

What three things did I do today to encourage my toddler's first words?

Examples: Did I use a particular strategy or technique? Did we play a certain game or perform a special play routine? Did I infuse language and purposefully use specific target words in my daily routines?

1 _____

_____

2 _____

_____

3 _____

> Embed language techniques into your daily routines, but also infuse them into those random yet shared events like a plane flying above, a knock at the door, or a sudden thunderstorm. These unplanned events provide many communication opportunities.

What did my toddler say or do in response to these three things?

Examples: My toddler looked at me, smiled, and tried to say, "Open" when I waited expectantly for him. My toddler gestured "all done" when she was finished playing with the playhouse. My toddler gave me his toy car when I said, "Oh, I like your car!"

1 _____

_____

2 _____

_____

3 _____

Could I have done or said anything differently?

Examples: Maybe I should have waited until I had my toddler's full attention before I expected him to follow my direction. Maybe I was talking too much and didn't give my child enough time to initiate communication. Perhaps my toddler did not have enough opportunities to hear the target word.

_____

_____

What will I do tomorrow to stimulate or further develop my toddler's first words?

Examples: Try a different strategy. Try the same strategy but do it consistently through my toddler's daily routines. Try a different play routine.

_____

_____

What questions or comments do I have for my toddler's speech-language pathologist, teacher, or other professional?

_____

_____

Day 19

Date_____

> Wonder is what makes life genuinely personal. Beauty is what triggers wonder. Wonder attunes to beauty through sensitivity and is unfolded by secure attachment. When wonder, beauty, sensitivity, and secure attachment are present, learning is meaningful.
>
> —Catherine L'Ecuyer, author of *Educate in Amazement*

What three things did I do today to encourage my toddler's first words?

Examples: Did I use a particular strategy or technique? Did we play a certain game or perform a special play routine? Did I infuse language and purposefully use specific target words in my daily routines?

1 _____

_____

2 _____

_____

3 _____

_____

What did my toddler say or do in response to these three things?

Examples: My toddler looked at me, smiled, and tried to say, "Open" when I waited expectantly for him. My toddler gestured "all done" when she was finished playing with the playhouse. My toddler gave me his toy car when I said, "Oh, I like your car!"

1 _____

_____

2 _____

_____

3 _____

_____

Could I have done or said anything differently?

Examples: Maybe I should have waited until I had my toddler's full attention before I expected him to follow my direction. Maybe I was talking too much and didn't give my child enough time to initiate communication. Perhaps my toddler didn't have enough opportunities to hear the target word.

_____

_____

What will I do tomorrow to stimulate or further develop my toddler's first words?

Examples: Try a different strategy. Try the same strategy but do it consistently through my toddler's daily routines. Try a different play routine.

_____

_____

What questions or comments do I have for my toddler's speech-language pathologist, teacher, or other professional?

_____

_____

_____

Day 20

Date_____

wWhat three things did I do today to encourage my toddler's first words?

Examples: Did I use a particular strategy or technique? Did we play a certain game or perform a special play routine? Did I infuse language and purposefully use specific target words in my daily routines?

It is a happy talent to know how to play.

—Ralph Waldo Emerson

1 _____

_____

2 _____

_____

3 _____

_____

What did my toddler say or do in response to these three things?

Examples: My toddler looked at me, smiled, and tried to say, "Open" when I waited expectantly for him. My toddler gestured "all done" when she was finished playing with the playhouse. My toddler gave me his toy car when I said, "Oh, I like your car!"

1 _____

_____

2 _____

_____

3 _____

_____

Could I have done or said anything differently?

Examples: Maybe I should have waited until I had my toddler's full attention before I expected him to follow my direction. Maybe I was talking too much and didn't give my child enough time to initiate communication. Perhaps my toddler didn't have enough opportunities to hear the target word.

_____

_____

_____

What will I do tomorrow to stimulate or further develop my toddler's first words?

Examples: Try a different strategy. Try the same strategy but do it consistently through my toddler's daily routines. Try a different play routine.

_____

_____

_____

What questions or comments do I have for my toddler's speech-language pathologist, teacher, or other professional?

_____

_____

_____

Day 21

Date_____

> When playing with your child, give him a chance to explore the toy and problem-solve how to play with it before showing him what to do.

What three things did I do today to encourage my toddler's first words?

Examples: Did I use a particular strategy or technique? Did we play a certain game or perform a special play routine? Did I infuse language and purposefully use specific target words in my daily routines?

1 _____

_____

2 _____

3 _____

_____

What did my toddler say or do in response to these three things?

Examples: My toddler looked at me, smiled, and tried to say, "Open" when I waited expectantly for him. My toddler gestured "all done" when she was finished playing with the playhouse. My toddler gave me his toy car when I said, "Oh, I like your car!"

1 _____

_____

2 _____

_____

3 _____

_____

Could I have done or said anything differently?

Examples: Maybe I should have waited until I had my toddler's full attention before I expected him to follow my direction. Maybe I was talking too much and didn't give my child enough time to initiate communication. Perhaps my toddler didn't have enough opportunities to hear the target word.

_____

_____

_____

What will I do tomorrow to stimulate or further develop my toddler's first words?

Examples: Try a different strategy. Try the same strategy but do it consistently through my toddler's daily routines. Try a different play routine.

_____

_____

_____

What questions or comments do I have for my toddler's speech-language pathologist, teacher, or other professional?

_____

_____

_____

Weekly Update

How Am I Doing?
How have I improved my ability to encourage communication, first words, and interaction with my toddler?

_____

_____

_____

_____

How Is My Toddler Doing?
How is my toddler becoming a more effective communicator? What new first words is he or she more regularly saying? Are any previously spoken words being said more frequently or with better clarity?

_____

_____

_____

_____

My Goals for Next Week:

I will work on using _____ (name of technique) during

_____ (name daily routine or

specific play activity) and will focus on having my toddler say or

do _____ _____ (selected target word

or other goal suggested by my speech-language pathologist).

Superstar Highlight from This Week!

It made me smile when

_____

_____

_____

_____

_____

Repetition is so important. I worked with a little boy who loved playing with balls but would not say the word "ball." His parents and I chose to target the word "ball." We threw, rolled, tossed, caught, and bounced balls and read every picture book we could find about balls. Jackson really enjoyed reading Kim Scanlon's picture book, Learning to Read Is a Ball. After systematically using various techniques, Jackson readily says, "Ball," to request and comment and is starting to combine ball with the words throw and my.

—Cindy, a pediatric speech-language pathologist

GOALS FOR WEEK 4

➽ My target word(s) for the week will be

_____

➽ Are these words developmentally appropriate and motivating to my toddler, and/or do they mesh well with our family dynamic?

☐ Yes ☐ No

➽ What will these words help my toddler to do? Circle the communicative function(s).

☐ Request ☐ Comment
☐ Reject or protest ☐ Ask questions
☐ Label ☐ Socially interact and connect

➽ What technique(s) will I practice this week to target this word/these words? Circle the technique(s).

☐ Identify and appreciate the child's lead ☐ Give choices
☐ Be responsive ☐ Imitate, imitate, imitate
☐ Pause in anticipation ☐ Create predictable play routines
☐ Set it up ☐ Strategically prompt for target words

➽ This week, I will embed the language technique(s) and focus on using the target(s) during the following daily routine(s):

☐ Going potty ☐ Getting ready for a nap
☐ Brushing teeth ☐ Sorting and washing laundry and folding clothes
☐ Washing hands
☐ Getting dressed ☐ Playing
☐ Preparing and eating a meal or snack ☐ Reading a book
☐ Taking a bath
☐ Getting ready to leave the house ☐ Getting ready for bed
☐ Getting into and riding in the car ☐ Other daily routine: _____
☐ Shopping at a store _____
☐ Going to _____ (name of destination) _____
☐ Changing diapers

WEEK 4: *"Remember to..." "My child loves when..." "I have to keep..."*

MONDAY

TUESDAY

WEDNESDAY

THURSDAY

FRIDAY

SATURDAY

SUNDAY

NOTES

Week 4: Day 22

Date_____

Did you know? A word learning study revealed that typically developing children usually have to be exposed to a new vocabulary word approximately thirteen times before understanding it while children with specific language impairment had to have about twenty-seven exposures. To say the new vocabulary words, the typically developing children needed more than twenty-three tries and the children with specific language impairment needed more than 49 tries.

Ricks, S.L. & Alt, M. (2016)

What three things did I do today to encourage my toddler's first words?

Examples: Did I use a particular strategy or technique? Did we play a certain game or perform a special play routine? Did I infuse language and purposefully use specific target words in my daily routines?

1 _____

_____

2 _____

_____

3 _____

_____

What did my toddler say or do in response to these three things?

Examples: My toddler looked at me, smiled, and tried to say, "open," when I waited expectantly for him. My toddler gestured "all done" when she was finished playing with the playhouse. My toddler gave me his toy car when I said, "Oh, I like your car!"

1 _____

_____

2 _____

_____

3 _____

_____

Could I have done or said anything differently?

Examples: Maybe I should have waited until I had my toddler's full attention before I expected him to follow my direction. Maybe I was talking too much and didn't give my child enough time to initiate communication. Perhaps my toddler didn't have enough opportunities to hear the target word.

_____

_____

What will I do tomorrow to stimulate or further develop my toddler's first words?

Examples: Try a different strategy. Try the same strategy but do it consistently through my toddler's daily routines. Try a different play routine.

_____

_____

What questions or comments do I have for my toddler's speech-language pathologist, teacher, or other professional?

_____

_____

Day 23

Date_____

What three things did I do today to encourage my toddler's first words?

Examples: Did I use a particular strategy or technique? Did we play a certain game or perform a special play routine? Did I infuse language and purposefully use specific target words in my daily routines?

> Repetition is the mother of all learning.
>
> —Latin Proverb

1 _____

_____

2 _____

_____

3 _____

_____

What did my toddler say or do in response to these three things?

Examples: My toddler looked at me, smiled, and tried to say, "Open" when I waited expectantly for him. My toddler gestured "all done" when she was finished playing with the playhouse. My toddler gave me his toy car when I said, "Oh, I like your car!"

1 _____

_____

2 _____

_____

3 _____

_____

Could I have done or said anything differently?

Examples: Maybe I should have waited until I had my toddler's full attention before I expected him to follow my direction. Maybe I was talking too much and didn't give my child enough time to initiate communication. Perhaps my toddler didn't have enough opportunities to hear the target word.

_____

_____

_____

What will I do tomorrow to stimulate or further develop my toddler's first words?

Examples: Try a different strategy. Try the same strategy but do it consistently through my toddler's daily routines. Try a different play routine.

_____

_____

_____

What questions or comments do I have for my toddler's speech-language pathologist, teacher, or other professional?

_____

_____

_____

Day 24

Date_____

Repetition is the key for any learning. When children are able to duplicate activities, the tasks become easier.

—KBYU Eleven, a viewer- supported public television service of Brigham Young University

What three things did I do today to encourage my toddler's first words?
Examples: Did I use a particular strategy or technique? Did we play a certain game or perform a special play routine? Did I infuse language and purposefully use specific target words in my daily routines?

1 _____

_____

2 _____

_____

3 _____

_____

What did my toddler say or do in response to these three things?
Examples: My toddler looked at me, smiled, and tried to say, "Open" when I waited expectantly for him. My toddler gestured "all done" when she was finished playing with the playhouse. My toddler gave me his toy car when I said, "Oh, I like your car!"

1 _____

_____

2 _____

_____

3 _____

_____

Could I have done or said anything differently?
Examples: Maybe I should have waited until I had my toddler's full attention before I expected him to follow my direction. Maybe I was talking too much and didn't give my child enough time to initiate communication. Perhaps my toddler didn't have enough opportunities to hear the target word.

_____

_____

_____

What will I do tomorrow to stimulate or further develop my toddler's first words?
Examples: Try a different strategy. Try the same strategy but do it consistently through my toddler's daily routines. Try a different play routine.

_____

_____

_____

What questions or comments do I have for my toddler's speech-language pathologist, teacher, or other professional?

_____

_____

_____

Day 25

Date_____

What three things did I do today to encourage my toddler's first words?

Examples: Did I use a particular strategy or technique? Did we play a certain game or perform a special play routine? Did I infuse language and purposefully use specific target words in my daily routines?

1 _____

_____

2 _____

_____

3 _____

_____

Did you know? Research supports that playing outdoors, particularly in a green space with lots of grass and trees, can improve your child's focus and attention. Toddlers often seem to have an endless supply of energy. Incorporate some green playtime into your child's daily routine.

(Faber & Kuo, 2011)

What did my toddler say or do in response to these three things?

Examples: My toddler looked at me, smiled, and tried to say, "Open" when I waited expectantly for him. My toddler gestured "all done" when she was finished playing with the playhouse. My toddler gave me his toy car when I said, "Oh, I like your car!"

1 _____

_____

2 _____

_____

3 _____

_____

Could I have done or said anything differently?

Examples: Maybe I should have waited until I had my toddler's full attention before I expected him to follow my direction. Maybe I was talking too much and didn't give my child enough time to initiate communication. Perhaps my toddler didn't have enough opportunities to hear the target word.

_____

_____

What will I do tomorrow to stimulate or further develop my toddler's first words?

Examples: Try a different strategy. Try the same strategy but do it consistently through my toddler's daily routines. Try a different play routine.

_____

_____

What questions or comments do I have for my toddler's speech-language pathologist, teacher, or other professional?

_____

_____

Day 26

Date_____

Curiosity drives learning. Spark your child's curiosity by encouraging discovery, following his or her interests, exposing him or her to new and interesting things, and modeling interest and excitement in the world around you.

What three things did I do today to encourage my toddler's first words?
Examples: Did I use a particular strategy or technique? Did we play a certain game or perform a special play routine? Did I infuse language and purposefully use specific target words in my daily routines?

1 _____

_____

2 _____

_____

3 _____

_____

What did my toddler say or do in response to these three things?
Examples: My toddler looked at me, smiled, and tried to say, "Open" when I waited expectantly for him. My toddler gestured "all done" when she was finished playing with the playhouse. My toddler gave me his toy car when I said, "Oh, I like your car!"

1 _____

_____

2 _____

_____

3 _____

_____

Could I have done or said anything differently?
Examples: Maybe I should have waited until I had my toddler's full attention before I expected him to follow my direction. Maybe I was talking too much and didn't give my child enough time to initiate communication. Perhaps my toddler didn't have enough opportunities to hear the target word.

_____

_____

_____

What will I do tomorrow to stimulate or further develop my toddler's first words?
Examples: Try a different strategy. Try the same strategy but do it consistently through my toddler's daily routines. Try a different play routine.

_____

_____

_____

What questions or comments do I have for my toddler's speech-language pathologist, teacher, or other professional?

_____

_____

_____

Day 27

Date_____

What three things did I do today to encourage my toddler's first words?

Examples: Did I use a particular strategy or technique? Did we play a certain game or perform a special play routine? Did I infuse language and purposefully use specific target words in my daily routines?

1 _____

_____

2 _____

_____

3 _____

_____

What did my toddler say or do in response to these three things?

Examples: My toddler looked at me, smiled, and tried to say, "Open" when I waited expectantly for him. My toddler gestured "all done" when she was finished playing with the playhouse. My toddler gave me his toy car when I said, "Oh, I like your car!"

1 _____

_____

2 _____

_____

3 _____

_____

Did you know? A recent study showed that toddlers and parents spoke less overall and had a less collaborative and engaging experience when reading a story using an electronic tablet as opposed to a print book. This may have occurred because the toddlers fixated on tapping and swiping the buttons on the tablet, which in turn required their parents to give more directions on how to use the tablet instead of making meaningful comments about the story line.

(Munzer, Miller, Weeks, Kaciroti, & Radesky, 2019).

Could I have done or said anything differently?

Examples: Maybe I should have waited until I had my toddler's full attention before I expected him to follow my direction. Maybe I was talking too much and didn't give my child enough time to initiate communication. Perhaps my toddler didn't have enough opportunities to hear the target word.

_____

_____

_____

What will I do tomorrow to stimulate or further develop my toddler's first words?

Examples: Try a different strategy. Try the same strategy but do it consistently through my toddler's daily routines. Try a different play routine.

_____

_____

What questions or comments do I have for my toddler's speech-language pathologist, teacher, or other professional?

_____

_____

Day 28

Date_____

> Free the child's potential, and you will transform him into the world.
>
> —Maria Montessori,
> Italian physician and educator

What three things did I do today to encourage my toddler's first words?

Examples: Did I use a particular strategy or technique? Did we play a certain game or perform a special play routine? Did I infuse language and purposefully use specific target words in my daily routines?

1 _____

_____

2 _____

_____

3 _____

_____

What did my toddler say or do in response to these three things?

Examples: My toddler looked at me, smiled, and tried to say, "Open" when I waited expectantly for him. My toddler gestured "all done" when she was finished playing with the playhouse. My toddler gave me his toy car when I said, "Oh, I like your car!"

1 _____

_____

2 _____

_____

3 _____

_____

Could I have done or said anything differently?

Examples: Maybe I should have waited until I had my toddler's full attention before I expected him to follow my direction. Maybe I was talking too much and didn't give my child enough time to initiate communication. Perhaps my toddler didn't have enough opportunities to hear the target word.

_____

_____

_____

What will I do tomorrow to stimulate or further develop my toddler's first words?

Examples: Try a different strategy. Try the same strategy but do it consistently through my toddler's daily routines. Try a different play routine.

_____

_____

_____

What questions or comments do I have for my toddler's speech-language pathologist, teacher, or other professional?

_____

_____

_____

Day 29

What three things did I do today to encourage my toddler's first words?

Examples: Did I use a particular strategy or technique? Did we play a certain game or perform a special play routine? Did I infuse language and purposefully use specific target words in my daily routines?

1 _____

_____

2 _____

_____

3 _____

_____

> Further facilitate your child's understanding of a new word by including actions, facial expressions, and gestures while saying the word. For example, if you say, "Yuck," stick out your tongue to show that you think something is repulsive, or if you say, "Tired," yawn and act tired.

What did my toddler say or do in response to these three things?

Examples: My toddler looked at me, smiled, and tried to say, "Open" when I waited expectantly for him. My toddler gestured "all done" when she was finished playing with the playhouse. My toddler gave me his toy car when I said, "Oh, I like your car!"

1 _____

_____

2 _____

_____

3 _____

_____

Could I have done or said anything differently?

Examples: Maybe I should have waited until I had my toddler's full attention before I expected him to follow my direction. Maybe I was talking too much and didn't give my child enough time to initiate communication. Perhaps my toddler didn't have enough opportunities to hear the target word.

_____

_____

_____

What will I do tomorrow to stimulate or further develop my toddler's first words?

Examples: Try a different strategy. Try the same strategy but do it consistently through my toddler's daily routines. Try a different play routine.

_____

_____

_____

What questions or comments do I have for my toddler's speech-language pathologist, teacher, or other professional?

_____

_____

_____

Day 30

Date_____

> It is paradoxical that many educators and parents still differentiate between a time for learning and a time for play without seeing the vital connection between them.
>
> —Dr. Leo Buscaglia, author and professor

What three things did I do today to encourage my toddler's first words?

Examples: Did I use a particular strategy or technique? Did we play a certain game or perform a special play routine? Did I infuse language and purposefully use specific target words in my daily routines?

1 _____

_____

2 _____

_____

3 _____

_____

What did my toddler say or do in response to these three things?

Examples: My toddler looked at me, smiled, and tried to say, "Open" when I waited expectantly for him. My toddler gestured "all done" when she was finished playing with the playhouse. My toddler gave me his toy car when I said, "Oh, I like your car!"

1 _____

_____

2 _____

_____

3 _____

_____

Could I have done or said anything differently?

Examples: Maybe I should have waited until I had my toddler's full attention before I expected him to follow my direction. Maybe I was talking too much and didn't give my child enough time to initiate communication. Perhaps my toddler didn't have enough opportunities to hear the target word.

_____

_____

_____

What will I do tomorrow to stimulate or further develop my toddler's first words?

Examples: Try a different strategy. Try the same strategy but do it consistently through my toddler's daily routines. Try a different play routine.

_____

_____

_____

What questions or comments do I have for my toddler's speech-language pathologist, teacher, or other professional?

_____

_____

_____

Weekly Update

How Am I Doing?
How have I improved my ability to encourage communication, first words, and interaction with my toddler?

_____

_____

_____

_____

How Is My Toddler Doing?
How is my toddler becoming a more effective communicator? What new first words is he or she more regularly saying? Are any previously spoken words being said more frequently or with better clarity?

_____

_____

_____

_____

My Goals for Next Week:

I will work on using _____ (name of technique) during

_____ (name daily routine or

specific play activity) and will focus on having my toddler say or

do _____ _____ (selected target word

or other goal suggested by my speech-language pathologist).

Superstar Highlight from This Week!

It made me smile when

_____

_____

_____

_____

_____

_____

This week I began to drastically limit my daughter's screen time. Honestly, it was a harder adjustment for me because I have to get things done and putting on the television or giving her my iPad was the easiest option. But, I can't believe the difference I see in her already! Marie has been playing more with her toys, staying with one toy for a longer time, and overall appears to be much calmer too! Since she's playing more with her toys, it's much more natural for me to join in and use a technique here and there. It makes me feel so much better knowing that I'm helping her more and more.

—Mother of Marie, aged thirty-three months

Hip hip hooray!
You completed the 30-Day Workbook!

Time to celebrate. It's amazing what can happen when your efforts
are focused and based on the best available guidance.

30-Day Recap

HOW DID I DO?

How have I improved my ability to encourage communication, first words, and interaction with my toddler? Please use the lines below to review your 30-day language-stimulation adventure.

I learned to

_____

_____

_____

_____

_____

_____

_____

_____

_____

I became better at

_____

_____

_____

_____

_____

_____

_____

_____

_____

_____

HOW DID MY TODDLER DO?

My toddler communicates more effectively by

_____
_____
_____
_____
_____
_____
_____

My toddler says the following words

_____
_____
_____
_____
_____
_____
_____

My toddler is using words to (What communicative functions are now being met?)

_____
_____
_____
_____
_____
_____
_____

My toddler is using words for a variety of communicative functions like

_____
_____
_____
_____
_____
_____
_____

WORDS OR WORD APPROXIMATIONS MY TODDLER SAYS

How has my toddler's vocabulary expanded this past month? Please fill in this chart after completing your 30-day language-stimulation adventure. Compare this completed chart with the chart in the beginning of the book.

Date_____

As of the above date, my toddler currently says the following words or word approximations independently and with no support or prompting from me:

TODDLER WORD PRODUCTION	TODDLER'S INTENDED WORD	TYPE OF WORD	COMMUNICATIVE FUNCTION
Wawa	Water	Noun	To request

MY GOALS FOR THE NEXT MONTH

> *All you need is the plan, the road map, and the courage to press on to your destination.*
>
> —Earl Nightingale

Our 30-day language-stimulation adventure has come to an end. It is my hope that *My Toddler's First Words* has carved out a fundamental plan to guide you into the future.

How will you continue?

_____

_____

_____

_____

_____

What do you hope to achieve next month?

_____

_____

_____

_____

_____

_____

What are your goals?

_____

_____

_____

_____

_____

_____

_____

I will work on using _____ (name of a technique) during

_____ (name daily routine or specific play routine) and

will focus on having my toddler say or do _____ _____ (selected

target word or other goal suggested by my speech-language pathologist).

Please continue to press on and enjoy the process.
I wish you and your child the very best.

Additional Notes

Reference List

A University Center for Excellence in Developmental Disabilities Education, Research, and Service. n.d. "Teaching First 'Words' [PDF file]. Retrieved from http://cdd.unm.edu/autism/pdfs/.

Armonia, A. C., L. C. Mazzega, F. C. Pinto, A. C. Souza, J. Perissinoto & A. C. Tamanaha. 2015. "Relationship between Receptive and Expressive Vocabulary in Children with Specific Language Impairment." *Revista CEFAC* 17 (3): 759–765. Epub June 2015. Retrieved from https://dx.doi.org/10.1590/1982-021620156214.

American Academy of Pediatrics. 2016. "American Academy of Pediatrics Announces New Recommendations for Children's Media Use." Retrieved from https://www.aap.org/en-us/about-the-aap/aap-press-room/pages/american-academy-of-pediatrics-announces-new-recommendations-for-childrens-media-use.aspx.

Blachowicz, C. L. Z. n.d. *Best Practices in Vocabulary Instruction.* Retrieved April 28, 2015, from https://perspective.pearsonaccess.com.

Carpenter, R. L., A. M. Mastergeorge, T. E. Coggins. 1983. "The Acquisition of Communicative Intentions in Infants Eight to Fifteen Months of Age." *Language and Speech*, 26: 101–116.

Chonchaiya, W. & C. Pruksananonda. 2008. "Television Viewing Associates with Delayed Language Development." *Acta Paediatrica* 97 (7): 977–982.

Core, C., E. Hoff, R. Rumiche & M. Senor. 2013. "Total and Conceptual Vocabulary in Spanish-English Bilinguals from 22 to 30 Months: Implications for Assessment." *Journal of Speech, Language, and Hearing Research* 56 (5): 1637–1649.

Duch, H., E. M. Fisher, I. Ensari, M. Font, A. Harrington, C. Taromino, C. Rodriguez. 2013. "Association of screen time use and language development in Hispanic toddlers: a cross-sectional and longitudinal study." *Clinical Pediatrics* 52 (9): 857–865.

Dunst, C. J., C. M. Trivette & D. W. Hamby. 2012. "Meta-Analysis of Studies Incorporating the Interests of Young Children with Autism Spectrum Disorders into Early Intervention Practices." *Autism Research and Treatment*: 1–10.

Eisenberg, S. 2004. "Structured Communicative Play Therapy for Targeting Language in Young Children." *Communication Disorders Quarterly* 26 (1): 29–35.

Faber, T. A. & F. E. Kuo. 2011. "Could Exposure to Everyday Green Spaces Help Treat ADHD? Evidence from Children's Play Settings." *Applied Psychology: Health and Well-Being* 3 (3): 281–303.

Fenker, D. & H. Schutze. 2008. "Learning by Surprise: Novelty Enhances Memory. That Fact Has Practical Implications for Educators." *Scientific American*. Retrieved from https://www.scientificamerican.com/article/learning-by-surprise/.

Fey, M. E., P. J. Yoder, S. F. Warren & S. L. Bredin-Oja. 2013. "Is More Better? Milieu Communication Teaching in Toddlers with Intellectual Disabilities." *Journal of Speech, Language, and Hearing Research* 56: 679–693.

Gershkoff-Stowe, L. & E. R. Hahn. 2007. "Fast Mapping Skills in the Developing Lexicon." *Journal of Speech, Language, and Hearing Research* 50: 682–697.

Gill, C., J, Mehta, K. Fredenburg, & K. Barklett. 2015. "Imitation Therapy for Non-Verbal Toddlers." *Child Language Teaching and Therapy* 27(1): 97-108.

Hadley, P. A., M. Rispoli & H. Ning. 2016. "Toddlers' Verb Lexicon Diversity and Grammatical Outcomes." *Language, Speech, and Hearing Services in Schools* 47: 44–58.

Haebig, E., A. McDuffie & S. E. Weismer. 2013. "Brief Report: Verbal Responsiveness and Language Development in Toddlers on the Autism Spectrum." *Journal of Autism and Developmental Disorders* 43 (9): 2218–2227.

Hill, A. 2011. "Singing to Children May Help Development of Language Skills" [web log post]. Retrieved from https://www.theguardian.com/lifeandstyle/2011/may/08/singing-children-development-language-skills.

Hoff, E. 2005. *Language Development* (3rd ed.). Belmont: Thomson Wadworth.

Kaiser, A. 2011. "KidTalk: Naturalistic Communication Intervention Strategies for Parents and Teachers of Young Children" [PDF file]. Retrieved from https://www.aucd.org/docs/SIG%20Docs/EIEC/Kaiser_Webinar_2_22_11.pdf

KBYU Eleven Organization. 2010. "Learning through the Early Years: The Benefits of Repetition and Variation" [PDF file]. Retrieved from http://www.kbyutv.org/kidsandfamily/readytolearn.

"Language Development in Children." n.d.. Retrieved from https://childdevelopmentinfo.com/child-development/language_development/.

Lanza, J. R. & L. K. Flahive. 2012. "LinguiSystems Guide to Communication Milestones" [PDF file]. Retrieved from https://www.linguisystems.com/pdf/Milestonesguide.pdf.

L'Ecuyer, C. 2014. "The Wonder Approach to Learning." *Frontiers in Human Neuroscience* 8: 1–8.

Lederer, S.H. 2018. "First words: Assessment and speech therapy goals" [online course]. In *Medbridge*. Retrieved from https://www.medbridgeeducation.com/courses/details/first-words-assessment-and-speech-therapy-goals-susan-h-lederer-speech-language-pathology-pediatrics

Lederer, S.H. 2018. "Intervention for single words through simple sentences"[online course]. In *Medbridge*. Retrieved from https://www.medbridgeeducation.com/courses/details/intervention-for-single-words-through-simple-sentences-susan-h-lederer-speech-language-pathology-pediatrics

Levy, A. 2013. "Why Children Learn Faster with Only a Few Books: Repeatedly Reading the Same Book to Toddlers Helps Them Learn New Words" [web log post]. Retrieved from http://www.dailymail.co.uk/news/article-2287648/Why-children-learn-faster-books-Repeatedly-reading-book-toddlers-helps-learn-new-words.html.

Light, J. & K. Drager. n.d. "Step 3: Select Appropriate Vocabulary." Retrieved from http://aackids.psu.edu/index.php/page/show/id/6/index.html.

Marton, K. & B. Gusztav. 2009. "Imitation of Body Postures and Hand Movements in Children with Specific Language Impairment." *Journal of Experimental Child Psychology* 102 (1): 1–13.

McMillan, B. T. M. & J. R. Saffran. 2016. "Learning in Complex Environments: The Effects of Background Speech on Early Word Learning." *Child Development*, 00 (0): 1–15.

Moore, H. 2016. "Naturalistic Communication Intervention with Young Children: How to Partner with Parents to Make Meaningful Differences in Children's Lives" [webinar]. In *Video Continuing Education*. Retrieved from http://course.videocontinuingeducation.com/ets/store/.

Moyses, K. 2012. "Movement can increase learning in children" [web log post]. Retrieved from http://msue.anr.msu.edu/news/movement_can_increase_learning_in_children.

Munzer, T.G, A.L., Miller, H.M., Weeks, N. Kaciroti, & J. Radesky. 2019. "Differences in Parent-Toddler Interactions With Electronic Versus Print Books." *Pediatrics* 143 (4): 1-10.

Nelson, K. 1973. "Structure and Strategy in Learning to Talk." *Monographs of the Society for Research in Child Development* 38: 1-140.

Newman, N. 2014. *Raising Passionate Readers: 5 Easy Steps to Success in School and Life*. New York: Tribeca View Press.

Northwestern University. 2013. "Language Acquisition: Nouns before Verbs?" *ScienceDaily*. Retrieved from http://sciencedaily.com/releases/2013/03/130325184020.htm.

Northwestern University. 2013. "Understanding How Infants Acquire New Words across Cultures." *ScienceDaily*. Retrieved from http://sciencedaily.com/releases/2013/09/130927123424.htm.

Reed, J., K. Hirsh-Pasek & R. M. Golinkoff. 2017. "Learning on Hold: Cell Phones Sidetrack Parent-Child Interactions." *Developmental Psychology* 53 (8): 1428–1436.

Ricks, S.L. & M. Alt. 2016. "Theoretical Principles to Guide the Teaching of Adjectives to Children Who Struggle with Word Learning: Synthesis of Experimental and Naturalistic Research with Principles of Learning Theory." *Language, Speech, and Hearing Services in Schools* 47: 181–190.

Risley, T. n.d. "Dr. Todd Risley: Meaningful Differences in the Language Learning Environments of Young American Children" (David Boulton, Interviewer) [YouTube video]. Retrieved from http://www. childrenofthecode.org/interviews/risley.htm.

Romeo, R. R., J. A. Leonard, S. T. Robinson, M. R. West, A. P. Mackey, M. L. Rowe & J. D. Gabrieli. 2018. "Beyond the 30-Million-Word Gap: Children's Conversational Exposure Is Associated with Language-Related Brain Function." *Psychological Science*: 1–11. https://doi.org/10.1177/0956797617742725.

Roseberry-McKibbin, C. & M. N. Hedge. 2006. *An Advanced Review of Speech-Language Pathology* (2nd ed.). Austin, TX: Pro-ed.

Sandhofer, C. & L. B. Smith. 2007. "Learning Adjectives in the Real World: How Learning Nouns Impedes Learning Adjectives." *Language Learning and Development* 3: 233–267.

Schwab, J. F. & C. Lew-Williams. 2016. "Repetition across Successive Sentences Facilitates Young Children's Word Learning." *Developmental Psychology* 52(6): 879–886.

Sigafoos, J., E. Drasgow, J. Reichle, M. O'Reilly, V. A. Green, & K. Tait. 2004. "Tutorial: Teaching Communicative Rejecting to Children with Severe Disabilities." *American Journal of Speech-Language Pathology* 13: 31–42.

Skwarecki, B. 2013. "Babies Learn to Recognize Words in the Womb" [web log post]. Retrieved from http://www.sciencemag.org/news/2013/08/babies-learn-recognize-words-womb.

Snow, C. E., S. Burns, P. Griffin. 1998. *Preventing Reading Difficulties in Young Children*. Washington, DC: National Academies Press.

Sosa, A. V. 2015. "Association of the Type of Toy Used during Play with the Quantity and Quality of Parent-Infant Communication." *JAMA Pediatrics* 170 (2): 132–138.

Sosa, A. V. & Stoel-Gammon, C. 2012. "Lexical and Phonological Effects of Early Word Production." *Journal of Speech, Language, and Hearing Research* 55: 596–608.

Tardif, T., P. Fletcher, W. Liang, Z. Zhang, N. Kaciroti & V. A. Marchman. 2008. "Baby's First 10 Words." *Developmental Psychology* 44(4): 929–938.

The Florida State University College of Medicine. n.d. "Our Evaluation Model." Retrieved from https://firstwords.fsu.edu/checklist.html.

"Toddle." *Merriam-Webster.com.* Merriam-Webster, n.d. Web. January 23, 2018.

Touhill, L. n.d.. "Interest-Based Learning" [PDF file]. Early Childhood Australia. Retrieved from https://www.earlychildhoodaustralia.org.au/nqsplp/wp-content/uploads/2012/06/NQS_PLP_E-Newsletter_No37.pdf.

University of Edinburgh. 2016. "Baby Talk Words with Repeated Sounds Help Infants Learn Language." *ScienceDaily.* Retrieved from http://sciencedaily.com/releases/2016/05/160527112647.html.

White, R. E. n.d. "The Power of Play: A Research Summary on Play and Learning" [PDF file]. St. Paul: Minnesota Children's Museum. Retrieved from http://www.childrensmuseums.org/images/MCMResearchSummary.pdf.

Woods, J. J., M. J. Wilcox, M. Friedman & T. Murch. 2011. "Collaborative Consultation in Natural Environments: Strategies to Enhance Family-Centered Support and Services." *Language, Speech, and Hearing Services in Schools* 42: 379–392.

Acknowledgements

Over the years, I have been blessed to treat toddlers who have amazingly dedicated parents and caregivers. It is and has been an honor to serve you and your families. Thank you for providing me the inspiration to write and create this book.

Completing this book would not have been possible without the support, feedback, and guidance from many individuals—several of whom I have never met in person.

Words cannot express how grateful I am for the following speech-language pathologists who wholeheartedly dove into my book, provided critical feedback, and shared their valuable insights and wisdom: Nancy Castignetti, MEd, MS, CCC-SLP; Laurie W. Peel, MA, CCC-SLP; Elisabeth Cuomo, MA, CCC-SLP; Jill Shook, MS, CCC-SLP; Megan Palasik, MS, CCC-SLP; and Anne Goff, MS, CCC-SLP. From the bottom of my heart, thank you.

Thank you to my friends, my early beta readers, who took time from their busy schedules to read earlier versions of this book and provide their honest, constructive feedback: Lindsay Grasso, Kelly DeLozier, Joe Cuomo, Susan DePasquale, and Dr. Nancy Barone. And thank you my countless friends on Facebook who voted to select this book's cover. Rocio Martin Osuna, your winning cover beat over two hundred different designs. Thank you so much for sharing your creativity and patience in designing the cover and all of the interior illustrations.

Throughout my career, I have had the opportunity to read research published in my industry's trade journals. Thank you to the American Speech-Language-Hearing Association (ASHA) for making it easy to access these journals so I could read articles, learn, and stay up to date on best practices.

The information I quote, summarize, and reference regarding language development theory was made possible by many professors, educators, and researchers. Thank you to each and every individual and institution listed in the references. Your contributions to our field are most meaningful. As a clinician, I have always felt more confident when citing research to validate my practices, explain a concept to a parent, or answer a question. For our field to thrive, we must continue to incorporate research into practice.

Above all, thank you to my dear family for all the love, encouragement, and patience. Although writing this book has been incredibly satisfying, it has not always been an easy process. Juggling the responsibilities of being a mother and a wife, my primary roles, along with having a speech therapy practice, many times left me too tired to read, reflect, and write. Passion to create a product that helps both families and professionals kept me going, however, it was not the only thing that drove me when I was exhausted. For your smiles and cuddles when I needed them most, I would like to thank my wonderful children, Kerrigan and Shane. I probably would not have finished this in a timely fashion if it wasn't for my husband, Ryan, always telling me to stay focused and to remember that it's a marathon, not a sprint. This saying always helped me to refocus and to redirect my energies.

I am also beyond grateful for my parents, who have always believed in me and encouraged me to do anything I wanted. Thank you for your unconditional love and for babysitting my sweeties when I needed to write, work, or sleep. I love you all.

About the Author

Kimberly Scanlon is a New Jersey–licensed speech-language pathologist who is nationally certified by the American Speech-Language and Hearing Association (ASHA). A creative thinker and passionate therapist who believes children should have fun in therapy, Kimberly is also the author of the best-selling book, *My Toddler Talks: Strategies and Activities to Promote Your Toddler's Language* and the unique interactive picture book, *Learning to Read is a Ball.*

Kimberly has had the opportunity to hone her skills by working in various settings serving all ages, populations, and disorders. She graduated from Rutgers University with a bachelor of science, earned her master of arts in communication disorders from Montclair State University, and is a four-time recipient of ASHA's ACE Award for continuing education. As the owner of Scanlon Speech Therapy LLC, a unique boutique practice in Bergen County, Kimberly embraces individuality and treats the whole person. Her goal is to spread compassion, hope, and speech and language tips one child at a time.

She enjoys reading, drinking coffee, taking long walks on the beaches of Long Beach Island, and spending time with her husband and two children. You can visit her website, www.mytoddlertalks.com, to learn about more speech and language tips, techniques, and activities.

Follow on Twitter at @ScanlonSpeech
Follow on Pinterest at My Toddler Talks
Find Scanlon Speech Therapy on Facebook

Other Books from the Author

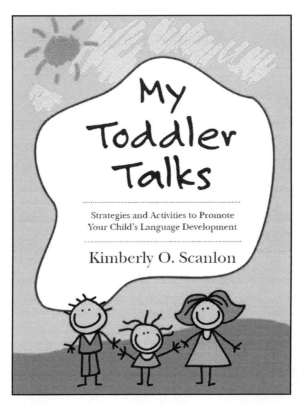

If you have enjoyed reading *My Toddler's First Words*, please share this book with others and consider writing a review on Amazon or Goodreads. I would love to know what you think. Thank you!